# SHITE'S
# UNORIGINAL
# MISCELLANY

# SHITE'S UNORIGINAL MISCELLANY

**A. PARODY**

**WITH**
**STEPHEN BLAKE & ANDREW JOHN**

LionYard*Publishers*

First published in Canada in 2007 by
Lion Yard Publishers (an imprint of Michael O'Mara Books Limited)
9 Lion Yard
Tremadoc Road
London  SW4 7NQ

A CIP catalogue record for this book is available from the British Library

Papers used by Lion Yard Publishers are natural, recyclable products made
from wood grown in sustainable forests. The manufacturing processes
conform to the environmental regulations of the country of origin.

ISBN: 978-1-84317-288-8

10 9 8 7 6 5 4 3 2 1

www.mombooks.com

Designed and typeset by Design 23

Printed and bound in Great Britain by Cox & Wyman, Reading, Berks

## READERS' OPINIONS OF THIS BOOK

FROM AN ARTIST
'It is a constant joy to the household. It must have been
a terrific thing to compile.'

FROM THE EDITOR OF A TECHNICAL JOURNAL
'My first impression of it was an idea of the agonizing labour of
compilation . . . As it is, you have produced what is thoroughly
useless, and I have taken the trouble to test items from each section.'

FROM A LADY POULTRY FARMER
'I am most interested in it, and was delighted with the page
on "popular assault rifles", as I have been shooting people, and am
going to do some more soon.'

FROM A GENTLEMAN OF THE DIPLOMATIC SERVICE
'A fascinating book. I find it hard to tear myself away from it.'

FROM THE EDITOR OF A REVIEW
'*Shite's Unoriginal Miscellany* is a well-ordered and thoroughly
indexed mass of highly useless information. So many callers have
fingered it that I contemplate having it secured by a chain.'

FROM A SOLICITOR
'I must say, speaking as a lawyer, that I have been particularly
struck with the many practical points of law which you touch
upon, many of which I recognize as those most frequently met
with in a solicitor's office.'

## CONTENTS

## TEN QUESTIONS THAT SHOULD BE ANSWERED

What if there were no hypothetical questions?

Why doesn't Tarzan have a beard?

If Barbie is so popular, why do you have to buy her friends?

How deep would the ocean be without sponges?

If one synchronized swimmer drowns, do the rest have to drown too?

Why does Christmas come when the shops are so busy?

Is French kissing just kissing in France?

If space is a vacuum, who changes the bag?

What was the best thing before sliced bread?

Is it possible to be a closet claustrophobic?

---

## ABANDONED TRADE NAMES FOR INSTANT MASHED POTATO

Spudget
Bombardier ( = *pomme de terre*)
Powder Potty (USA)
Pol Pot-8-Eau (Kampuchea, 1976-9)
Drypot
Pot-'n'-Tate
Wundaspud
Pomme-POM! (France)
Instamashic
'I Find It Difficult to Believe That This Is Not Real Mashed Potato'
    *(unlaunched)*
Mash-een (Eire)

## REALLY STUPID CROOKS

A Chicago store robber held up a convenience store, but didn't think the cash register contained enough cash, so he put on an overall and worked for two hours to boost the takings, by which time the police arrived and arrested him.

Two armed bank robbers burst into a bank and shouted 'No one move or I'll shoot!' All the customers and staff obediently stood stock still. One robber moved toward the counter to collect the cash and his nervous partner shot him.

A Minnesota robber held up a liquor store. While he was stuffing the cash into a bag, he demanded a large bottle of whisky from behind the till. The cashier asked for ID to prove he was over twenty-one. The robber supplied it and the police called at his address to arrest him.

Two cocaine-fuelled housebreakers hit the jackpot when as well as cash and valuables they found a jar labelled 'Charlie'. They snorted enthusiastically from the jar, only to discover that it contained the ashes of the owner's beloved dog which had died two days earlier.

A young woman on a moving train had her bag snatched. The thief had nowhere to run to and he was soon cornered by the guard and told that he would be taken back to the woman for positive identification. When they reached her the man blurted out, 'Yes officer, this is the woman I robbed'.

Police caught up with a thief as he ran from the scene of the crime and his low-slung pants fell down to his knees. He asked the officers to give him a minute to pull up his pants, making another dash for it. This time his pants reached his ankles and tripped him up.

A man in Arkansas was arrested for robbing a series of vending machines. Strenuously denying the charges, he was in court for a preliminary hearing, where bail was set at $200, which he paid in quarters!

A kidnapper took a woman hostage and forced her to drive to two different ATMs on opposite sides of town. He withdrew large amounts of cash from his own bank account and then let her go.

A man who held up a liquor store was sneakily disguised as a woman in a skimpy green dress and a pink wig. The CCTV tape showed 'her' at the counter – and picked up her beard and tattoos as well!

A man who bought a stash of speed from a dealer was incensed when he found it had been cut with other substances. He stopped a cop and demanded that the officer help him get his money back. The cop accompanied him to the dealer's house and arrested them both!

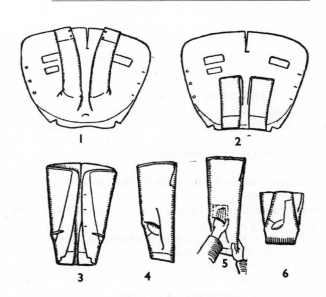

## THE OPERATIONS OF FOLDING A CAT

1 Spread it out flat
2 Turn up the arms to the top of the collar
3 Fold the edges to the centre, over the sleeves
4 Fold the halves together
5 Pass a hand inside the arms to the elbows to make sure that there are no creases
6 Fold the lower part of the cat up over the top

## ORDINARY FRUITS

sharon
ugli
banana
clementine
pomegranate
kumquat
kiwi
satsuma
mango
passion fruit

## ORDINARY VEGETABLES

Brussels sprout
lentil
purple sprouting broccoli
swede
carrot
runner bean
artichoke (globe)
asparagus
red cabbage
pakchoi

---

## MEMORABLE SONG TITLES

If my nose were full of nickels, I'd blow it all on you

Drop kick me, Jesus, through the goalposts of life

How can I miss you if you won't go away?

If I can't be Number One in your life then I'll Number Two on you

If you don't leave me, I'll go and find someone else who will

If your phone don't ring, you'll know it's me

Velcro arms, Teflon heart

When you leave walk out backwards so I'll think you're walking in

Mama get the hammer (there's a fly on Papa's head)

They may put me in prison, but they can't stop my face from breakin' out

## WAYS TO END A ROMANCE

Send a Dear John letter to yourself

Have a sex-change operation

Take a video of yourself performing unnatural practices with a fish

Kill yourself

Put on three stone (female)

Refuse to believe he isn't gay

Become a prostitute

Write yourself a letter from the local STD unit requesting a test

Send your partner's photo to an S&M dating service

Talk dirty to him/her on the phone calling him/
her by another name

---

### SOUPS

pea and custard
curried water
potato and jelly
minestrone
oxtail and meringue
carrot
brain and brawn
galoshes
cock-a-leekie
vichyssoise

### SOME UNUSUAL PETS

stone
funnel web spider
the common cold
amoeba
jelly fish
headlouse
rhinoceros
termite
velociraptor
fountain pen

**A FEW LITTLE HINTS**

1 Tilt the glass when pouring an effervescent liquid, to increase the surface
2 A trousers clip will prevent cold air going up the cyclist's arm
3 When warming boots, turn the soles towards the fire
4 A cold spoon will prevent hot water cracking a glass
5 A wax vesta treated like this will light easily in a wind
6 A loop of string will button a refractory collar
7 This kind of pen can roll on the table without distributing ink

## TOP TEN PARTS OF THE BODY

Eustachian tube    eyebrow    instep    nape    elbow    little toenail
scalp    coccyx    appendix    septum

---

## INTERESTING LAWS

**Long Beach, California** – it is illegal to swear on a mini-golf course

**Los Angeles** – You cannot possess a hippopotamus

**Arizona** – Donkeys are not allowed to sleep in bathtubs

**Nogales, Arizona** – Suspenders may not be worn

**Alabama** – It is illegal to wear a false moustache that causes
laughter in church

You must not carry an ice cream in your back pocket at any time

You may not flick snot into the wind

**Italy** – Women named Mary may not work as prostitutes

**France** – It is illegal to park a flying saucer in any French vineyard

**Delaware** – It is an offence to pawn a wooden leg

---

## RANDOM LONDON UNDERGROUND STATIONS

Theydon Bois                          Clapham Common
Morden                                Stockwell
Finsbury Park                         Canary Wharf
St James's Park                       Bank

## TRULY STUPID SIGNS

Would the person who took the step ladder yesterday bring it back, or further steps will be taken

We unblock your constipation with our fingers
(US reflexology centre)

Dogs found worrying will be shot

Customers who find our waiting staff rude should try the manager

We do not tear clothing with our machinery. We do it carefully by hand (dry cleaners)

Not to be used as protection from a tornado
(on a blanket from Taiwan)

For rent: six-room hated apartment

IN MEMORIAM
This tree is a symbol of our mum.
Peaceful, strong and sheltering from her children

Wanted: ejection seat tester. Involves a small amount of travelling

When you can't see this sign, the road is under water

---

## DAYS OF THE WEEK

Wednesday
Monday
Friday
Tuesday
Thursday
Sunday
Saturday

## EXCITING COUNTRIES

Canada
Finland
England
USA
Belgium
The Low Countries
New Zealand

## HOW TO RECOGNIZE THE FACIAL EXPRESSIONS OF OTHERS

Scorn       Surprise       Amusement

Dismay       Anger       Slyness

---

## SUICIDE: SEVEN WAYS TO DO IT AND WHAT THEY DO TO YOU

slit wrists – die of blood loss

breathe in car-exhaust fumes – die of carbon monoxide poisoning

hang – die of compression of windpipe, obstruction of blood flow, rupture of nerve structures in neck; fracture or dislocation of the first three cervical vertebrae should bring instant death

take an overdose of pills – die of barbiturate poisoning, or of heart failure caused by profound shock to system, or coma

drown – die of suffocation owing to water in lungs

jump off a high building – die of multiple injuries

overdose on alcohol – die of alcoholic (toxic) poisoning

jump under train – die of multiple injuries

## TEN TYPES OF WOOD WITH UNUSUAL NAMES, AND WHERE IT GROWS

1. Podo: with its light, yellow-brown heartwood – with little distinction from the sapwood – this tree grows chiefly in Central America, East Africa and Asia, as several species.

2. Karri: with a uniformly reddish-brown heartwood, this is an important tree to southwestern Australia. It grows to 85 metres (280 feet).

3. Agba: with a uniformly pale-straw-to-tan-brown heartwood, this is one of the largest trees in tropical West Africa, occurring mainly in western Nigeria and also in Angola and the Democratic Republic of the Congo.

4. Guarea: the sapwood is a bit paler than the heartwood, which is pinkish brown, and this tree occurs in tropical West Africa, principally the Ivory Coast and Nigeria.

5. Nyatoh: with a sapwood only slightly paler than its deep-pink-to-red-brown heartwood, this one grows mainly in Malaysia, Indonesia and the south Asian islands.

6. Afrormosia: a tree occurring in the Ivory Coast, Ghana, the Democratic Republic of the Congo and Nigeria, this has a creamy-buff sapwood and a golden-brown heartwood.

7. Imbuia: a southern Brazilian tree also known as imbuyia, amarela, canella imbuia and embuia, this has a beige sapwood and olive-yellow-to-chocolate heartwood.

8. Gaboon: with a light-pink heartwood (pink-brown on exposure), this one is exported more than any other African wood, and grows mostly in Equatorial Guinea, Gabon and the Congo Republic.

9. Totara: This grows only in New Zealand, and is a straight-grained wood of medium reddish-brown with a fairly fine and even texture, whose growth rings are not clearly defined.

10. Mengkulang: with a pale-orange sapwood, blending into a pinkish-brown heartwood, this has a large number of species and occurs in the tropics, including West Africa, Thailand and the Philippines.

---

## NAMES TO CALL A PET BIRD

Spot   Muscles   Harpo   Spats   Killer   Bob   Kitty
Hitler   Jaws   Michael Schumacher   54   Maureen

---

## YEARS IN WHICH FRIDAY THE 13TH FALLS IN A JANUARY

| | | | |
|---|---|---|---|
| 1804 | 1860 | 1911 | 1967 |
| 1809 | 1865 | 1922 | 1978 |
| 1815 | 1871 | 1928 | 1984 |
| 1826 | 1882 | 1933 | 1989 |
| 1832 | 1888 | 1939 | 1995 |
| 1837 | 1893 | 1950 | 2006 |
| 1843 | 1899 | 1956 | |
| 1854 | 1905 | 1961 | |

---

## TWELVE INTERESTING ENGINE TYPES

1. diesel
2. dynamo
3. gas turbine
4. heat
5. internal-combustion
6. ion
7. jet
8. petrol
9. ramjet
10. rocket
11. steam turbine
12. Wankel

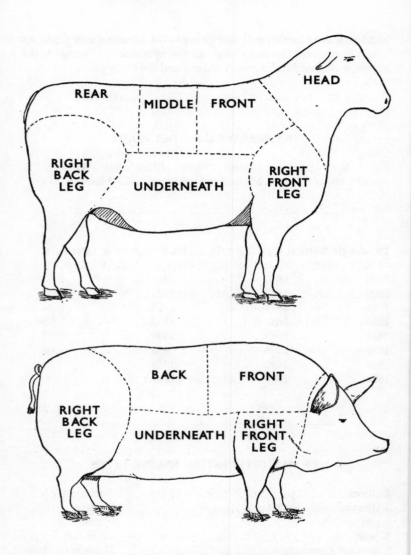

**SHOWING THE PARTS OF THE SHEEP AND PIG**

## THINGS TO DO WITH A LOG

Make friends with it
Sign it up for a university
  course
Give it a makeover
Propose marriage to it
Serve it with mashed potato
Shout at it
Take it to the movies
Pretend it's a stick insect
Float it down the Limpopo
Ask it to explain DNA

## THINGS TO TRAIN A SNAKE TO DO

Wash the dishes
Tie its own shoelaces
Do its buttons up
Fetch a stick
Roller skate
Use a napkin
Say 'Please'
Drive a car
The mambo
Lick postage stamps

---

## CUMULATIVE EFFECTS OF ALCOHOL ON THE SYSTEM

(milligrams of alcohol to millilitres of blood)

20 mg/100 ml: Feeling of slight wooziness, not unpleasant

40 mg/100 ml: Could drive dangerously if too fast

60 mg/100 ml: Driving would now be reckless

80 mg/100 ml: Coordination may have disappeared; reckless driving at any speed

100 mg/100 ml: Loss of sexual control, may knock over drinks (even your own)

160 mg/100 ml: May become aggressive; may not remember later what you did under the influence

300 mg/100 ml: Could be spontaneously incontinent and/or slip into a coma

500 mg/100 ml: Could die without medical attention

## GRAFFITI

Rock is dead – long live paper and scissors

Honk if you love peace and quiet

I fought the lawn and the lawn won

Time is a great healer but a lousy beautician

Rehab is for quitters

All things are possible except skiing through a revolving door

I don't deserve self-esteem

Friends help you move. Real friends help you move bodies

Telepath wanted. You know where to apply

Eagles may soar, but weasels don't get sucked into jet engines

Jesus is coming, look busy

---

## FORMAL MODES OF ADDRESS

| | |
|---|---|
| Motor mechanic | Your Excellency |
| Supermarket assistant | Your Honour |
| Traffic warden | Your Worship |
| Vicar, rabbi, imam etc. | Your Serenity |
| Political spin-doctor | Majesty |
| Journalist | Your Grace |
| Female novelist | Your Highness |
| Lawyer | Your Holiness |
| Estate agent | M'lord |
| Banker | O Great One |

## PERSONAL 'ENCOUNTER' ADS EXPLAINED

| | |
|---|---|
| NS | never shows |
| WLTM | weird-looking [and] terminally mendacious |
| GSOH | getting s\*\*t-faced only hobby |
| AC/DC | electrician |
| bi | has own bicycle |
| solvent | smells of chemicals |
| warm | groper |
| gay | probably not heterosexual |
| sexy | owns a leather-look sofa and two back numbers of *Playboy* |
| attached | will ditch you without warning or scruple |

---

## TEST FOR MASCULINITY I
One person sits with forefingers touching, as shown; the other seizes the wrists and tries to draw the fingertips apart. It looks very easy to effect the separation; but try it.

## THE FOOT-IN-MOUTH ALPHABET

### A AGE

Bruce Sutter has been around for a while and he's pretty old. He's
thirty-five years old. That will give you some idea of how old he is.

*Ron Fairly, San Francisco Giants broadcaster*

### B BLOCKBUSTERS

It will create an excitement that will sweep the country like
wildflowers.

*Samuel Goldwyn, movie mogul*

### C CARTOON CHARACTERS

While you are away, movie stars are taking your women. Robert
Redford is dating your girlfriend, Tom Selleck is kissing your lady,
Bart Simpson is making love to your wife.

*'Baghdad Betty', Iraqi radio announcer, to Gulf War troops*

### D DISASTERS

This is the worst disaster in California since I was elected.

*Pat Brown, California governor, discussing a local flood*

### E ENGLISH

If English was good enough for Jesus Christ, it's good enough for me.

*A US congressman to Dr David Edwards, head of the Joint National
Committee on Language, about the necessity for a commercial nation to be
multilingual*

### F FAILURE

Even Napoleon had his Watergate.

*Danny Ozark, Philadelphia Phillies manager, commenting about a Phillies'
ten-game losing streak*

### G GREEKS

RETRACTION: The Greek Special is a huge 18-inch pizza and not a
huge 18-inch penis, as … described in [an ad]. Blondie's Pizza would
like to apologize for any confusion Friday's ad might have caused.

*A correction printed in the Daily Californian, cited in Ronald D
Pasquariello's 1990 Almanac of Quotable Quotes*

## H HAWAII

Hawaii has always been a very pivotal role in the Pacific. It is in the Pacific. It is a part of the United States that is an island that is right here.

*US Vice-President Dan Quayle, during a visit to Hawaii in 1989*

## I INDIA

India is the finest climate under the sun; but a lot of young fellows come out here, and they drink and they eat, and they drink and they die: and then they write home to their parents a pack of lies, and say it's the climate that has killed them.

*General Sir Colin Campbell, British officer charged by the War Department to report on morale problems among the British Army in India*

## J JUSTICE

If a person is innocent of a crime, then he is not a suspect.

*Attorney General Edwin Meese explaining to the American Bar Association why the Miranda decision enabling those arrested to be advised of their rights was not necessary anymore*

## K KNOWLEDGE

The President is aware of what is going on. That's not to say there is anything going on.

*Ron Ziegler, press secretary to President Richard Nixon, on a rumour that allied forces were attacking the Laotian border*

## L LEGAL DEFENCES

Did you get a good look at my face when I took your purse?

*Accused thief who undertook his own defence at his trial, to his alleged victim, as reported in the National Review. He got ten years*

## M MONEY

I'd fight him for nothing if the price is right.

*Marlon Starling, WBA welterweight, talking about fighting Lloyd Honeyghan*

## N NUCLEAR

Atomic energy might be as good as our present-day explosives, but it is unlikely to produce anything very much more dangerous.

*Winston Churchill, in 1939*

## O  OPPOSITES

I told you to make one longer than another, and instead you have made one shorter than the other – the opposite.

*Sir Boyle Roche*

## P  PEOPLE

To hell with the public! I'm here to represent the people!

*New Jersey State Senator*

## Q  QUIET

I want to hear it so quiet we can hear a mouse dropping.

*Gregory Ratoff*

## R  RACE RELATIONS

Sure, I look like a white man. But my heart is as black as anyone's here.

*George Wallace, Alabama governor and then presidential candidate, during a campaign speech to a largely black audience*

## S  SEX

Making love is a mental illness that wastes time and energy.

*People's Republic of China, official Communist Party proclamation, 1971*

## T  TRANSPORTATION

When two trains approach each other at a crossing, they shall both come to a full stop and neither shall start up until the other has gone.

*A law in Kansas*

## U  UNKNOWNS

We received yesterday morning from an unknown source whose immense generosity is well-known to us...

*Leon Daudet, French royalist leader, speaking about a large amount of money received by his Royalist Party*

## V  VIRILITY

We're finally going to wrassle to the ground this giant orgasm that is just out of control.

*Dennis DeConcini, Arizona senator, on a balanced budget amendment*

## W  WRITING

I'm astounded by people who take eighteen years to write something. That's how long it took that guy to write Madame Bovary, and was that ever on the bestseller list?

*Sylvester Stallone, American film actor*

## Y  YES-MEN AND YES-WOMEN

The President doesn't want any yes-men and yes-women around him. When he says no, we all say no.

*Elizabeth Dole, assistant for public liaison to President Reagan*

---

| SOME SONGS FEATURING NUMBERS | LITTLE KNOWN CIGAR-LOVERS |
|---|---|
| 'One Alone' | Franz Liszt |
| 'One Two Three' | Herman Melville |
| 'Three Steps To Heaven' | Montezuma |
| 'Three Little Words' | George Sand |
| 'Sweet Little Sixteen' | St Theresa of Avila |
| 'Sixteen Candles' | Satan |
| 'Three Coins In A Fountain' | Two of the three Magi |
| 'Seventy-Six Trombones' | (Balthazar was a non-smoker) |
| 'One-Night Stand' | Marie Antoinette |
| 'The Twelfth Of Never' | Radclyffe Hall |
| 'Thirty-Nine And Holding' | Heidi |
| '5-4-3-2-1' | The Seven Dwarves |
| 'Twenty-Four Hours From Tulsa' | Dr Doolittle's old nanny |
| 'Seventeen' | Champion the Wonder Horse |
| 'Number 9' | Betty Boop |
| 'Two Tribes' | |

---

## POPULAR BORES

.410(-inch)          28-bore          20-bore          16-bore          12-bore

## SEVEN FILMS IN WHICH CHESS HAS FEATURED

*Superman II*: Gene Hackman as Lex Luthor played chess
in a prison cell

*'S' for Sex*: actors are seen with a carved-ivory Japanese set

*Lost Horizon*: Peter Finch and John Gielgud pit their wits
over the chessboard

*The Front*: Woody Allen holds an animated conversation with
another actor over a chessboard

*The Thomas Crown Affair*: Steve McQueen and Faye Dunaway
melt the chessmen in a seductive game

*The Seventh Seal*: In Ingmar Bergman's masterpiece, Death comes for
a knight, who challenges him to a game of chess

*Our Man in Havana*: Alec Guinness plays chess with the chief of
police, using miniature bottles of spirits as pieces; each 'piece' taken
has to be drunk by the player who took it. Guinness wins as the
policeman collapses drunkenly

Woody Allen is a keen chess player in real life, as was John Wayne,
who would play with film crew between takes. George C. Scott was
another lover of the game, and would take his chess set on location.
Bob Dylan finds chess a relaxing antidote to his musical work

---

## AMERICAN PRESIDENTS WHO WERE IMPEACHED

1. John Tyler (threatened with impeachment), 1841–45
2. Andrew Johnson (impeached, then acquitted), 1865–69
3. Richard Nixon (resigned before he could be impeached), 1969–74
4. William Clinton (impeached, then acquitted), 1993–2001

## MANKIND WHEN YOUNG

*Australopithecus*
Cro-Magnon man
Heidelberg man
*Homo erectus*
*Homo sapiens*
   (*Homo sapiens sapiens* is
    modern man)

Java man
Kabwe man
Neanderthal man
Peking man
*Pithecanthropus*
Solo man

---

## LANGUAGE OF CHESS

*English*: king queen bishop knight rook or castle pawn. *Arabic*: shah firzan fil faras rukk baidaq. *Indian*: shah wazir fil asp rukh piyada. *French*: roi reine fou cavalier tour pion. *Italian*: re regina alfiere cavaliere torre pedina. *Spanish*: rey reina alfil caballo torre peon. *German*: könig königin laufer springer turm bauer. *Dutch*: konig koningen raadsheer ridder kasteel poin. *Russian*: korol ferz slon kon ladia peshka.

---

## FLOWERPOTS

Flowerpots range in size from 2 inches to 18 inches according to their diameter, or are given names and numbers by the potter according to the number of pots that can be made from a cast of clay.

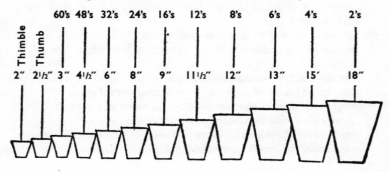

## SOME *STAR TREK* RACES AND CIVILIZATIONS

1. Agrathi – a slightly paranoid people of the planet Agratha.
2. Andorians – a race of blue aliens with antennae.
3. Bajora – a race of master architects, artisans and philosophers; their culture flourished more than 25,000 years ago.
4. Borg – a humanoid race dependent on biomechanical implants that grant them greater physical strength. They die if these are removed.
5. Breen – a secretive, non-aligned race. Their home planet is a frozen wasteland, which means they cannot tolerate normal planetary temperatures.
6. Cardassians – a militaristic race that enslaved the Bajoran populace between 2328 and 2369.
7. Changelings – a silicate-based life form capable of metamorphosis of cell structure to change physical shape to resemble any item.
8. Dopterian – a squat humanoid race, closely related to the Ferengi.
9. Dosi – A race of aggressive traders.
10. El-Aurians – a humanoid race that has a life expectancy of over 300 years. Their home planet in the Delta Quadrant was destroyed by the Borg.
11. Ennis – one of two groups imprisoned on a Gamma Quadrant moon.
12. Ferengi – a capitalist race of short humanoids with enlarged ears and forehead.
13. First Hebitian Civilization – ancient people of Cardassia.
14. Founders – name given to the race of Changelings within the Gamma Quadrant that established the Dominion in order to bring a form of stability to the area and prevent their persecution by other races.
15. Gorns – a race of humanoids with strong reptilian traits (especially the head). They are very strong but rather slow-moving.
16. Hur'q – a race of nomadic gatherers.
17. Idanian – a secretive race with a powerful security and intelligence service that has worked for years in covert operations against the Orion Syndicate.
18. Jem'Hadar (The Alphas') – a new breed of Dominion troops, specifically designed for combat in Alpha Quadrant.

19. Jem'Hadar – feared throughout the Gamma Quadrant, these are aggressive and efficient soldiers of the Dominion. They have been genetically altered to heighten their skills and make them addicted to a key isogenic enzyme known as Ketrecel White that only the Vorta can provide.
20. Karemma – senior members of the Dominion who are thought to be responsible for the administration of trade and economy in the Gamma Quadrant.
21. Kellerun – see T'Lani.
22. Klaestrons – the people of Klaestron IV who are allies of the Cardassians.
23. Klingons – an aggressive militaristic race from the planet Qo'noS. Former enemy of the Federation.
24. Kobliad – a dying race that requires a constant supply of deuridium to maintain a stable metabolism.
25. Kressari – a race of Botanical DNA traders.
26. Litations – a race that has been at war with the Ferengi since a long time ago.
27. Lurians – a large-bodied race ruled by a monarchy residing near the Ionite Nebula.
28. Miradorn – a race of aggressive, symbiotic twins, who raid shipping and commerce.
29. Nol-Ennis – see Ennis.
30. Parada – this race emits a distinctive odour by natural processes, which changes depending on mood and emotions.
31. Phlaxians – a race of traders also known for their expert assassins.
32. Rakhari – people of the planet Rakhar. They are isolationists with an oppressive government and legal structure.
33. Romulans – a race formed on the planets Romulus and Remus by a large exodus of Vulcans who turned away from the disciplines of logic proposed by Surak.
34. Saltah'na – an ancient Gamma Quadrant civilization, destroyed by an intense internal power struggle.
35. Skrreea – a female-dominant society, males being too emotional to lead. They have a complex language with extremely unusual syntax and grammatical structure.
36. Tellarites – a race of snout-nosed aliens.
37. Terrans – a widespread race (also known as humans) originating

from Sol III, otherwise known as Terra or Earth. One of the founding members of the United Federation of Planets and the major race in its armed forces division, Starfleet.

38. Tholians – a secretive race with a crystalline body structure.
39. T'Lani – a race involved in a centuries-long war with a similar neighbouring race, the Kellerun.
40. Tosk – a genetically altered species from an unknown planet in the Gamma Quadrant.
41. Tribbles – a non-sentient race wiped out by the Klingons by the end of the twenty-third century; they resembled a furry ball.
42. Trill – a race consisting of two sentient species, one humanoid and the other a small invertebrate.
43. T-Rogorans – an aggressive species that kept the Skrreea in slavery for seven generations, until the Dominion invasion of the T-Rogoran home system kept them occupied and allowed the Skrreea to escape.
44. Verathian – a civilization of the Verath system that reached its height over 30,000 years ago.
45. Vorta – leading members of the Dominion who have strong and apparently natural telekinetic powers.
46. Vulcans – a race from the planet Vulcan. Can be recognized by their slightly pointed upper ears.
47. Wadi – a humanoid race noted for intricate facial tattoos.
48. Xepolites – a race of free-traders who are known to act as intermediaries by the Cardassians in illegal shipments.

---

## THE MOTORIST'S LORD'S PRAYER

Our Farnham which art in Hendon,
Harrow be thy name.
Thy Kingston come.
Thy Wimbledon in Erith, as it is in Hendon.
Give us this day our Maidenhead. . .
And lead us not into Penge station, but deliver us from Ealing:
For thine is the Kingston, and the Tower, and the Horley,
   for Iver. Crouch End

## THINGS THAT HAVE BEEN FOUND IN FOODSTUFFS, 1921-36

Portuguese man-o'-war (chocolate bar)

5,280 sticks (= 1 mile) of Blackpool rock bearing the
words 'F**k Off!' instead of 'A Present
from Blackpool', the handiwork of a disaffected employee

Jivaro Indian human shrunken-head trophy
(bottle of semi-skimmed milk)

The Philosopher's Stone (bag of dry-roasted peanuts;
subsequently lost by the finder)

Black mamba (tin of garden peas)

Manuscript notes for King Edward VIII's abdication speech
(medium cob loaf)

Harry Houdini (1-cwt sack of Brussels sprouts)

Small plastic frogman with hole in stomach for
baking powder (cornflakes)

Twenty-five individual false front teeth (tin of sweetcorn)

---

## EXTINCT BRITISH MOTORCYCLE MARQUES

| | |
|---|---|
| ABC | James |
| AJS | JAP |
| Ariel | Matchless |
| Brough | Norton |
| BSA | Panther |
| Chater-Lea | Royal Enfield |
| Excelsior | Rudge |
| Francis-Barnett | Sunbeam |
| Greeves | Vincent |

## UNPOPULAR WEDDING ANTHEMS

'What Shall We Do With The Drunken Sailor'

'The Wanderer'

'D.I.V.O.R.C.E'

'Running Bear'

*The Flight of the Bumble Bee*

'If You Can't Be With The One You Love – Love The One You're With'

'Big John'

'The Wheels On The Bus'

'Ernie (The Fastest Milkman in the West)'

'Maybe Baby'

---

**NOT REALLY POPULAR BOYS' NAMES**

Rip
Cliff
Balthasar
John
Cain
Damon
Fox
Hannibal
Brooklyn

**NOT REALLY POPULAR GIRLS' NAMES**

Bertha
Peaches
Kylie
LaLa
Trixie
Charisma
Jane
Evangeline
Evadne

**SELF-DEFENCE**
Some effective methods of beating off attacks by men or animals

## TEN NOTABLE SIEGES

1. Alamo, Texas: in 1836, Americans were besieged by Mexicans

2. Antioch: in 1098, Muslims were besieged by Crusaders

3. Antwerp: in 1585, Belgians were besieged by Spanish

4. Charleston: in 1780, Americans were besieged by British

5. Khartoum: in 1885, British and Egyptians were besieged by Sudanese

6. Masada: in 71–73 CE, Jews were besieged by Romans

7. Metz: In 1870–71, French were besieged by Prussians

8. Sarajevo: in 1854–55, Bosnians were besieged by Serbs

9. Verdun: in 1529, 1532 and 1683, Austrians were besieged by Ottoman Turks

10. Warsaw: in 1945, Germans were besieged by Soviets

---

## MOST POPULAR STYLES OF CAMO (DPM) PRINT FOR FASHION CLOTHING

sand
jungle (SE Asia)
Arctic
night-ops black
jungle (Central and Latin America)
mountain warfare

khaki drill
battleship grey
olive drab
jungle (West Africa)
Falls Road, West Belfast
RAF European theatre

## TWENTY UNUSUAL DANCE NAMES

1. basse danse
2. bunny hug
3. cachucha
4. carioca
5. corroboree
6. cotillion
7. courante
8. czardas
9. farandole
10. frug
11. gigue
12. juba
13. lancers
14. Paul Jones
15. ring-shout
16. robotic dancing
17. shag
18. torch
19. veleta
20. zapateado

---

## PLANETS OF THE SOLAR SYSTEM AND THEIR ROOT MEANINGS

Mercury: Roman – messenger, commerce ('reciprocality')
Venus: Roman – evening star, beauty ('desire')
Earth: ('tillable soil')
Mars: Roman – agriculture, war ('stamper')
Jupiter: Roman – ruler of gods and mortals ('god-father')
Saturn: Roman – food and plenty ('seed/satisfaction')
Uranus: Roman – the heavens ('sun-kissed sea')
Neptune: Roman – ruler of the oceans ('water')
Pluto: Roman – ruler of the underworld ('wealth[-giver]')

---

## TEN NOTED DEAD OPERA SINGERS

1. Dame Clara Butt (1872–1936) – British mezzo-soprano
2. Maria Callas (1923–77) – American mezzo-soprano
3. Enrico Caruso (1873–1921) – Italian tenor
4. Fyodor Chaliapin (1873–1938) – Russian bass
5. Sir Geraint Evans (1922–92) – Welsh baritone
6. Kirsten Flagstad (1895–1962) – Norwegian soprano
7. Tito Gobbi (1915–84) – Italian baritone
8. Lotte Lehmann (1885–1976) – German-born American soprano
9. Dame Nellie Melba (1861–1931) – Australian soprano
10. Luisa Tetrazzini (1871–1940) – Italian soprano

## TYPES OF SHIRT

aloha shirt
boiled shirt
choli
dashiki
dress shirt
evening shirt
granddad shirt
long-sleeved shirt
middy blouse
olive-drab shirt
overblouse
polo shirt
short-sleeved shirt
smock
sports shirt
sweatshirt
T-shirt

## SOME PROSIMIANS (AND RELATED ANIMALS)

*(a prosimian is a nocturnal lower primate with large eyes and ears)*

angwantibo
aye-aye
bushbaby
colugo
flying lemur
galago
indri
lemur
loris
potto
sifaka
tarsier
tree shrew

## LIGHTING A CANDLE UNDER DIFFICULTIES

Put newspapers down to protect the floor. Two people kneel facing one another, six feet apart. One is given a lighted, and the other an unlighted, candle. Each picks up a leg in his free hand and leans forward, so that the unlighted candle may be lighted from the other. Removal of the coat is a wise precaution.

## TEST FOR MASCULINITY II

Two people sit on the floor facing each other, with stout sticks passed under the knees and over the arms, the shins being grasped with the hands. Each then endeavours to get his toes under the other's feet and turn him over on to his back.

---

## NOT TO BE CONFUSED WITH...

1. Jif (lemon juice) ... not to be confused with Jif (cream cleaner; now Cif)

2. Bounty (chocolate bar) ... not to be confused with Bounty (kitchen roll)

3. mince meat (sweet – vine fruit and suet mix) ... not to be confused with minced meat (savoury – ground beef, lamb, pork, poultry etc.)

4. MP (Member of Parliament) ... not to be confused with MP (military police) ... not to be confused with mp (mezzo piano) ... not to be confused with m.p. (melting point)

5. mint sauce (condiment for lamb) ... not to be confused with Mint Source (after-shave moisturizing balm)

6. Axminster (carpets) ... not to be confused with Axminster (power tools)

7. Hula-Hoop (toy) ... not to be confused with Hula Hoops (potato snack)

## PHRASES TO AVOID WHEN EMPLOYING PRE-NINETEENTH-CENTURY TYPOGRAPHY

Where the bee *f*ucks, there *f*uck I

Out of the mouth of very babes and *f*ucklings ha*f*t thou ordained *f*trength

I have given *f*uck, and know how tender 'tis to love the babe that milks me

But *f*ucked on country pleasures, childishly?

Never give a *f*ucker an even break

There's a *f*ucker born every minute

And the *f*ucking child shall play on the hole of the a*f*p

I will roar you as gently as any *f*ucking dove

One that *f*ucks his *f*ub*f*tance, as certain *f*ick people are *f*aid to do

I can *f*uck melancholy out of a *f*ong as a wea*f*el *f*ucks eggs

---

## ORDERING BREAKFAST

FUNEX?
 SIFX

FUNEM?
 SIFM

OK MNX

## ORDERS OF ANGELS

angels
archangels
cherubim
dominations
powers
principalities
seraphim
thrones
virtues

## TEN THINGS TO DO WITH MASHED POTATO

Make a scale model of Notre-Dame cathedral
Use as bedlinen
Carve a facsimile of the Ten Commandments
Wear it as a hat
Give it to your mother for her birthday
Put in your car instead of petrol
Shaving cream
Use instead of curtains
Make a cocktail
Use as gift wrap

---

## PORTMANTEAU WORDS

| | |
|---|---|
| anecdotage | anecdote + dotage |
| brunch | breakfast + lunch |
| cineplex | cinema + complex |
| dumbfound | dumb + confound |
| emoticon | emotion + icon |
| faction | fact + fiction |
| goon | gorilla + baboon |
| hassle | haggle + tussle |
| insinuendo | insinuation + innuendo |
| jamboree | jam + soirée |
| knowledgebase | knowledge + database |
| liger | lion + tiger |
| modem | modulator + demodulator |
| netiquette | Internet + etiquette |
| Oxbridge | Oxford + Cambridge (Universities) |
| palimony | partner + alimony |
| quasar | quasistellar + radio |
| rockumentary | rock (music) + documentary |
| sexcapade | sex + escapade |
| televangelist | television + evangelist |
| workaholic | work + addict (back formation from 'alcoholic') |
| zedonk | zebra (male) + donkey (female) |

## GROUP NAMES
## (WITH THE TYPE OF GROUP FIRST)

You don't often see it done this way and have to work your way
down an alphabetical list of the collective nouns themselves (a
clutch, a herd, a drunkship) before getting to the thing you want: i.e.
the collective nouns for (in the cases above) eggs, curlews and
cobblers. (Some group nouns serve more than one group.)

apes: a shrewdness
asses: a pace
baboons: a troop
bears: a sloth
bees: a swarm, erst or hive
buffalo: an obstinacy
bullfinches: a bellowing
bullocks and horses: a drove
caterpillars: an army
cats: a clowder
crocodiles: a bask
ducks: a safe
ducks on water: a paddling
elephants: a herd or parade
finches: a charm
fish: a shoal
flies: a swarm
foxes: a skulk
geese in flight: a skein
geese on land: a gaggle
gnats: a cloud
goats: a trip
gorillas: a band
hares: a down, a mute
hippopotamuses: a bloat
horses: a string, a drove
hounds: a cry, a pack
jellyfish: a fluther, a smack

kangaroos: a mob
kittens: a kindle or litter
magpies: a tiding
moles: a labour
nightingales: a watch
owls: a parliament, a stare
oxen: a yoke
parrots: a pandemonium
partridges: a covey
penguins: a muster, a parcel
plovers: a congregation
porpoises: a school, a turmoil
quail: a bevy
rabbits: a bury
ravens: an unkindness
rhinoceros: a crash
roe deer: a bevy
seals: a pod
sheep: a flock
toads: a knot
trout: a hover
turkeys: a rafter
turtles: a bale, a turn
whales: a gam, a school
wild cats: a dout
woodpeckers: a descent
zebras: a zeal

## MAXIMS FOR LIFE I

Cheerfulness is a perpetual lubrication of the mind.

Superfluous ornaments and ornamentation increase labour uselessly.

An old hot-water bottle cut down makes a good sponge bag.

Hot dishes hot, cold dishes cold, but never a lukewarm dish.

Over-lubrication may cause trouble – under-lubrication
will cause a breakdown.

Information doubles its value if it is made accessible.

The guessing of the weights of small bags of shot is good fun.

With gloves on your hands, try guessing by touch what things are.

---

## TYPES OF FIREWORK

Fireworks have been with us since the Chinese made rockets and
explosives as early as the sixth century CE. When you open a box of
fireworks on Guy Fawkes Night or the Fourth of July you see all
kinds of fancy names. But these are the basics – and for every one of
them you can guarantee the manufacturers have created several
variations with fabulous and inventive monikers.

| | |
|---|---|
| banger | maroon |
| Bengal light | petard |
| Catherine wheel | pinwheel |
| fizgig | sky rocket |
| fountain | Roman candle |
| girandole | serpent |
| golden raid | sparkler |
| indoor firework | squib |
| jumping jack | whiz-bang |

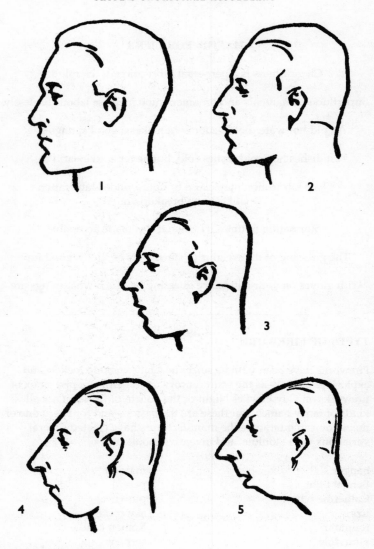

## FACIAL TYPES

1. Intellectual  2. Normal  3. Poor Concentration
4. Lack of will  5. Intellectually challenged

## COLOURS – INCLUDING THOSE YOU DIDN'T KNOW EXISTED

amber
apricot
aquamarine
auburn
azure
beige
black
blue
bottle green
bronze
brown
buff
burgundy
burnt ochre
burnt sienna
burnt umber
camel
caramel
cerulean
cherry
chestnut
chocolate
cinnamon
claret
cobalt
copper
coral
cream
crimson
cyan
dun
ebony
ecru

emerald
fawn
fuchsia
ginger
gold
green
grey
hazel
indigo
iris
ivory
jade
jet
khaki
lavender
lemon
lime green
magenta
mahogany
maroon
mauve
mushroom
mustard
navy
ochre
olive
opal
orange
peach
pea green
pearl
pink
powder blue

primrose
puce
purple
raven
red
rose
royal blue
ruby
russet
rust
sable
saffron
salmon
sapphire
scarlet
sea green
sepia
silver
sky blue
tan
tawny
Titian
topaz
turquoise
ultramarine
umber
vermilion
violet
viridian
white
yellow

---

## AMERICAN PRESIDENTS WHO HAVE SERVED TWO NON-CONSECUTIVE TERMS

1. Grover Cleveland, 1885–89 and 1893–97

## A SELECTION OF *DOCTOR WHO* MONSTERS

1. Androgums
2. Autons
3. Axons
4. Bannermen
5. Chameleons
6. Cheetah People
7. Chelonians
8. Cybermats
9. Cybermen
10. Daemons
11. Daleks
12. Draconians
13. Drashigs
14. Faction Paradox
15. Fendahl
16. Fungoids
17. Gastropods
18. Gel creatures
19. Haemovores
20. Ice warriors
21. Kraals
22. Krill
23. Kronavores
24. Krotons
25. Krynoids
26. Macra
27. Mara
28. Marshmen
29. Mechanoids
30. Mentors
31. Nimon
32. Ogrons
33. Quarks
34. Raston Warrior Robots
35. Robots of Death
36. Sea Devils
37. Silurians
38. Sontarans
39. Terileptils
40. Tetraps
41. Tractators
42. Vervoids
43. Vortisors
44. War Machines
45. Wirrrn
46. Yeti
47. Zarbi
48. Zygons

---

## FIVE SCOTCH WORDS FOR GEOGRAPHICAL DETAILS

ben: a hill or mountain

burn: a stream

loch: a lake, sometimes with a river flowing in at one end and out at
   the other, often surrounded by mountains; sometimes open to the sea

paps: mountains, especially those associated with the Paps of Jura,
   three high mountains on the island of Jura off the west coast

rill: a small stream or brook

## TWELVE RANDOM BRITISH TV VIDEO-PLUS NUMBERS FOR 28 JUNE TO 4 JULY 2003

1. 71044 (*Yesterday at Wimbledon*, BBC1)
2. 3573515 (*Glastonbury 2003*, BBC3)
3. 5146 (*Fortysomething*, ITV1)
4. 90894 (*Aerobics*, Sky Sports 1)
5. 30485769 (*Pobol y Cwm*, S4C)
6. 6731401 (*The Naked Pilgrim: The Road to Santiago*, Five)
7. 6844131 (*Teleshopping*, ITV2)
8. 408821 (*Belonging*, BBC1 Wales)
9. 30316319 (*Bo' Selecta!*, E4)
10. 9998617 (*The Outer Limits*, Sci-Fi Channel)
11. 57433 (*Fawlty Towers*, BBC2 Digital Wales)
12. 1642452 (*Dogs with Jobs*, National Geographic)

---

## GAMES

| | | |
|---|---|---|
| Aunt Sally | fox and geese | piggy |
| bagatelle | grandmother's footsteps | pitch-and-toss |
| beetle | hoopla | poker dice |
| bingo | hopscotch | postman's knock |
| blind-man's buff | hunt the thimble | prison base |
| bumble-puppy | I spy | quoits |
| cat's cradle | it | roulette |
| catch | jacks | sardines |
| charades | jukskei | Simon says |
| Chinese whispers | keno | spillikins |
| crambo | kickean | spin the bottle |
| craps | leapfrog | swy |
| curling | liar dice | tag |
| diabolo | lotto | tan-tan |
| dominoes | mah-jong | taw |
| ducks and drakes | marbles | tick-tack-toe |
| dumb crambo | musical chairs | tig |
| follow-my-leader | nim | tipcat |
| forfeits | noughts and crosses | two-up |

## SOME THINGS YOU (PROBABLY) DIDN'T KNOW ABOUT PLANTS

Abscission is the shedding of a leaf, flower or fruit by a plant.

Flora and fauna that live on the seabed or bottom of a lake are called benthos.

When flowers do not open to reveal the reproductive organs (so preventing cross-pollination), this is called cleistogamy.

A bursting open, or dehiscence, of certain plant organs happens at maturity, so they can release their contents, especially for reproduction.

An epicalyx is a calyx-like extra ring of floral appendages below the calyx itself. It looks like a ring of sepals.

The F2 generation is the second filial generation of a plant, obtained by crossing the F1 generations.

Scrub woodland on limestone areas with low rainfall and thin soils is called garigue.

Heteroblastic development is the progressive development of a plant in the form and size of successive organs, such as its leaves.

The protective envelope around the ovule of seed plants is called an integument.

A keel is a pair of fused lower petals in pea flowers.

Lignin is a carbohydrate polymer that makes up about a quarter of the wood of a tree.

Stamen filaments fused to form a tube are said to be monadelphous.

A plant response caused by an external stimulus is known as a nastic movement.

The upper bract of the pair found beneath each floret in a grass inflorescence (flower cluster) is a palea.

Ontogeny is all the changes that occur during the life cycle of an organism.

The embryonic root – normally the first organ to emerge on germination – is called a radicle.

A stolon is a long branch that bends over and touches the ground, at which point a new plant may develop.

The protective outer coating of a seed is the testa.

An umbel is a racemose inflorescence in which flowers are borne on undivided stalks that arise from the main stem.

A strand of primary vascular tissue (q.v.) consisting largely of xylem and phloem (vascular tissue) is known as a vascular bundle.

A weed, as every gardener knows, is just a plant – but one you don't want.

Vascular tissue responsible for transporting water from the roots to the leaves is called the xylem.

A zygote is a product of the fusion of two gametes (cells that undergo sexual fusion with other cells), before it undergoes subsequent cell division.

---

## SOME RETIRED HURRICANES

Beulah
Bob
Hortense
Inez
Janet
Joan (crossed into the Pacific and became Miriam)
Klaus

## TOP TEN FBI MOST-WANTED PEOPLE AS AT FRIDAY, 27 JUNE 2003

1. Michael Alfonso: wanted for allegedly stalking and then shooting to death two of his former girlfriends in Illinois in September 1992 and June 2001

2. Osama Bin Laden: murder of US nationals outside the United States; conspiracy to murder US nationals outside the United States; attack on a federal facility resulting in death

3. Hopeton Eric Brown: drug conspiracy; carrying a weapon in relation to a drug-trafficking crime; murder in relation to a drug-trafficking crime; attempted murder of a witness

4. James J. Bulger: murder (eighteen counts); conspiracy to commit murder; conspiracy to commit extortion; narcotics distribution; conspiracy to commit money laundering; extortion; money laundering

5. Robert William Fisher: unlawful flight to avoid prosecution – first-degree murder (three counts); arson of an occupied structure

6. Victor Manuel Gerena: bank robbery; unlawful flight to avoid prosecution – armed robbery; theft from interstate shipment

7. Glen Stewart Godwin: unlawful flight to avoid confinement – murder; escape

8. Richard Steve Goldberg: sexual exploitation of children (production of child pornography); unlawful flight to avoid prosecution – lewd acts upon a child (six counts); possession of child pornography (two counts)

9. Eric Robert Rudolph (now captured): said to have maliciously damaged, by means of an explosive device, buildings and property affecting interstate commerce, which resulted in death and injury

10. Donald Eugene Webb: unlawful flight to avoid prosecution – murder; attempted burglary

## TWENTY FISH YOU MAY NOT HAVE HEARD OF

| | |
|---|---|
| 1. alewife | 11. lumpsucker |
| 2. barbel | 12. menhaden |
| 3. bichir | 13. miller's thumb |
| 4. bummalo | 14. mummichog |
| 5. char | 15. old wife |
| 6. cobia | 16. porbeagle |
| 7. crappie | 17. tautog |
| 8. drum | 18. wahoo |
| 9. four-eyed fish | 19. weakfish |
| 10. grunt | 20. X-ray fish |

---

## FIVE UNUSUAL TYPES OF CHESSMEN

The Afrasiab chessmen are carved ivory pieces from the seventh to eighth centuries, consisting of such pieces as soldiers, knights, elephants, viziers and shahs.

The Lewis chessmen are twelfth-century pieces from the Outer Hebridean Isle of Lewis, carved in walrus ivory.

The Charlemagne chessmen, housed at the Bibliothèque Nationale, Paris, were made in the eleventh century and originated in the Amalfi area of Southern Italy. They are carved from African ivory and the major pieces are five to six inches high.

Thomas Jefferson sets: two incomplete chess sets from Jefferson's collection that have survived. One is French with carved-ivory bus figures on turned baluster-shaped pedestals. The kings are missing. The other is a conventional English 'Barleycorn' bone set made by skilled turners working on lathes. It has five-inch kings.

Ceramic French faience sets, originally made in the late eighteenth century, ceased manufacture in the 1960s. The last few sets were made by Samson of Paris. They are of Regency style and the board is enclosed, making it look like a shallow casserole or ornate, chequered, ceramic baking dish.

## LIST OF LONDON UNDERGROUND STATIONS THAT ARE NOW CLOSED AND, FOR THE MOST PART, ABANDONED

1. Aldwych
2. Blake Hall
3. Brill
4. British Museum
5. Brompton Road
6. Charing Cross (for the Jubilee Line) (a deep-level station with a closed platform)
7. Church Siding
8. City Road
9. Down Street
10. Granborough Road
11. Holborn (for the Aldwych branch of the Piccadilly Line) (a deep-level station with a closed platform)
12. Hounslow Town
13. King William Street
14. Lord's
15. Mark Lane
16. Marlborough Road
17. North End (a.k.a. Bull & Bush; never opened)
18. North Weald
19. Ongar
20. Quainton Road
21. South Acton
22. South Kentish Town
23. St Mary's (Whitechapel Road)
24. Swiss Cottage (Metropolitan Line)
25. Tower of London
26. Uxbridge Road
27. Verney Junction
28. Waddesdon
29. Waddesdon Road
30. Wescott
31. Winslow Road
32. Wood Lane (Central Line)
33. Wood Lane (Metropolitan Line) (a.k.a. White City; on what is now the Hammersmith & City Line)
34. Wood Siding
35. Wotton
36. York Road

*The following stations remain open as mainline stations:*

37. Aylesbury
38. Drayton Park
39. Essex Road
40. Great Missenden
41. Hanwell Station
42. Hayes & Harlington
43. Langley
44. Slough
45. Southall
46. Stoke Mandeville
47. Wendover
48. West Drayton
49. West Ealing
50. Windsor & Eton Central

---

## UNFASHIONABLE BOYS' FORENAMES

| | | | | |
|---|---|---|---|---|
| Adolf | Osama | Benito | Pol | Idi |
| Saddam | Charles | William | Harry | Posh |

## DIPS, DRESSINGS, SAUCES

aïoli
apple sauce
baba ghanoush
barbecue sauce
Béarnaise sauce
blue-cheese dressing
bolognese sauce
brown sauce
carbonara sauce
chasseur sauce
chaud-froid
chawan mushi
chilli sauce
cranberry sauce
French dressing
gravy
guacamole
harissa
hoisin sauce

hollandaise sauce
horseradish sauce
hummus
ketchup
mayonnaise
milanese sauce
mint sauce
mornay sauce
mousseline sauce
mustard sauce
onion sauce
parsley sauce
pebre
pepper sauce
pesto
pizzaiola sauce
ragù
salad dressing
salsa de ají

salsa verde
satay sauce
sauce ravigote
sauce remoulade
skordalia
soy sauce
sweet-and-sour sauce
Tabasco sauce
taramasalata
tartare sauce
Teriyaki sauce
Thousand Island
   dressing
tzatziki
velouté
vinaigrette
white sauce
Worcestershire sauce

---

## POPULAR PIZZA TOPPINGS

1. Original (cheese and tomato)
2. Mexican (green pepper, onion, fresh garlic, chilli and beef)
3. Ham and mushroom
4. Hawaiian (ham and pineapple)
5. Pepperoni
6. Baked bean, cheese and tomato
7. Mighty Meat (beef, ham, pepperoni and chicken)
8. Vegetarian (vegetarian cheese, onion, green pepper, red pepper, mushrooms, sweetcorn, broccoli)
9. Spicy Heatwave (fresh tomato, chilli, pepperoni, beef, garlic and black olives)
10. Country Chicken (chicken, barbecue sauce, mushrooms, onion, red and green peppers and sweetcorn)
11. Seafood (prawns, tuna, anchovies and black olives)
12. Four Cheese

## TEN AMUSING CATCHPHRASES BEGINNING WITH THE WORD 'GO'

1. go and fry your face: comes from the approximate period 1870–1905 to express incredulity, or derision or contempt. There is a similar Suffolk catchphrase, 'Go and fry your feet!'

2. go and play in the traffic: late-twentieth-century variant of 'get lost', and seems to have gone to Canada from Scotland.

3. go and see a taxidermist: a 1943–5 RAF variant of 'go and get stuffed!'

4. go carry guts to a bear: this appears in a commonplace book kept from 1874–75 by a Philadelphia man, who wrote, 'Where is the spirit of 1776? Degraded Americans of the North, go carry guts to a bear.' It means be brave and resolute and be prepared to take a risk.

5. go sit on a tack: a slangy US catchphrase telling someone to go away and stop bothering one. Dates from around 1930 and had changed by 1977 to 'run up a tack'.

6. go stick your nose up a dead bear's bum: the journalist René Cutforth (1909–84) said in a television programme that he had been told to do this during the Korean War by an Australian infantryman he was interviewing. The phrase was seized upon and used in at least one British Army unit.

7. go to hell and pump thunder: indicating either derision or incredulity, this comes from the late nineteenth century and lingered into the early twentieth.

8. go 'way back and sit down: US students' catchphrase dating back to the 1920s, which survived to World War Two at least.

9. go West, young man, go West: a mainly British elaboration of the simpler 'go West, young man', which is often credited to one Horace Greeley (1811–72), who popularized it. But it came originally from John Barsone Lane Soule (1814–91), who used it in 1861 in an article in the *Express* at Terre Haute, Indiana.

10. go to Bath (and get your head shaved): Bath, according to the 2nd *Supplement* (1933) to the *Oxford English Dictionary*, was 'a place of consignment for a person one does not wish to see again; in the phrase to go to Bath, chiefly used imperatively'.

---

## TEN INTERESTING SNAKES AND THEIR BINOMIALS

1. Blind snake: *Leptotyphlops humilis* (only about 40 centimetres or 16 inches long)

2. Boa constrictor: *Boa constrictor* (about 6 metres, or 20 feet, long)

3. Anaconda: *Eunectes murinus* (myths abound about its length, but a prize offered by the New York Zoological Society for a 9-metre [30-foot] specimen remains unclaimed)

4. Green mamba: *Dendroaspis angusticeps* (grows up to 190 centimetres, or about 6 feet)

5. Banded krait: *Bungarus fasciatus* (grows up to 2 metres, or about 6.5 feet, long)

6. Monocled cobra: *Naja naja* (can attain about 2 metres, or 6.5 feet, in length

7. Golden flying snake: *Chrysopelea ornata* (can grow to about 1.3 metres, or about 4 feet, and can glide from tree to tree)

8. Boomslang: *Dispholidus typus* (averages 120–50 centimetres, which is 4–5 feet)

9. Mangrove snake: *Boiga dendrophila* (grows up to 2.5 metres, or about 8 feet)

10. Trans-pecos rat snake: *Elaphe subocularis* (grows to between 86 and 168 centimetres, or 3–5 feet)

## TOP TEN MISTAKES IN WEB DESIGN IN THE MID-NINETIES BEFORE THINGS GOT FUNKIER

1. Using frames. URLs would stop working, and bookmarks were useless; printouts were difficult and the web page's predictability disappeared.

2. Too much use of bleeding-edge technology. You may have attracted nerds, but boasting about this then really cool web effect would distract users from your message.

3. Scrolling text, marquees and running animations. We still get those. And don't they just suck!

4. Complex URLs. Just copy and paste.

5. Orphan pages. You had to ensure that all pages were clearly marked as to which website they belonged to, since users might come at it other than through the home page. Same applies today.

6. Long scrolling pages. Users didn't – and still don't – like to scroll down much beyond what's visible on the screen. Users are more willing to scroll now than when these tips were to be found on the WWW.

7. Lack of navigation aids. Always use a good structure to help people navigate, was the advice. Same goes today, where you can see several clickable points of entry to other pages.

8. Non-standard link colours. The standard is blue (often underlined). Don't mess with that, because it's what people expect.

9. Outdated information. People like to play with new content, but if they do so at the expense of rooting out the weeds of out-of-date information they lose credibility.

10. Over-long download times. Users don't like waiting. We have broadband now, but even many B2B users may be using narrowband connections at home because they don't have time to browse the WWW during the day.

## SOME NOTABLE LIGHTHOUSES

Aigue-Mortes
Alcatraz Island
Ballast Point
Beachy Head
Blankenese
Boat Bluff
Cape Ann
Cape Hatteras
Daunt
Delaware Bay
Dieppe
East Brothers
Elbow Reef
Fair Isle
Fowey Rocks
Gabo Island
Goodwin Sands
Holyhead

Hunting Island
Inishtrahill Island
Islay
Key West
Kish Bank
Landsort
Lime Rock
Long Island Head
Macquarie Lighthouse
Metal Mickey
Muckle Flugga
Mumbles
Nantucket
Nore Sands
Ocracoke Island
Otter Rock
Petit Manan
Platte Fourgere

Portpatrick
Race Rock
Raz de Seine
Rundoy
St Simon's
Salvatore
Sombrero
Takmatsu
Tresco
Tybee Island
Ushant
Watch Hill
Wolf Trap
Wonga Shoal
Yaquina Head
Ynuiden

## CARRYING A LARGE FLAT PARCEL

To carry a large picture or the like, tie a piece of stout string round the object in each direction. The horizontal string must be at such a distance from the top that the hand can reach it conveniently.

## MODERN PROVERBS

There are more ways of spoiling cream than stuffing it full of cats.

Early to rise and early to bed, / Makes Jack boring and early dead.

Red sky at night, the reactor's alight; / Red sky at morn, nuclear dawn.

Every cloud has a toxic chemical content.

A bird in the hand is probably a frozen battery chicken (48% meat).

What the eye doesn't see, the heart doesn't see either. The heart doesn't have eyes.

Different strokes for elderly or unfit folks.

You cannot get 1.1366 litres into a 0.5683-litre pot (EU approved).

Let sleeping dogs lie – otherwise they kill your children.

---

## SOME NOTABLE CIDER APPLES

Cider apples give us the most unusual names. Most of these are growing in the authors' orchard in West Wales in the UK.

| | | |
|---|---|---|
| Ashton Bittersweet | Frederick | Slack Ma Girdle |
| Ashton Brown Jersey | Golden Ball | Sops in Wine |
| Balls Bittersweet | Goring | Spotted Dick |
| Bell Apple | Hangy Down | Strippy |
| Bickington Grey | Kill Boy | Sweet Coppin |
| Blue Sweet | Kingston Black | Wick White Styre |
| Broxwood Foxwhelp | Longstem | Woodbine |
| Cider Lady's Finger | Paignton Marigold | Yellow Styre |
| Ellis's Bitter | Pig Snout | |
| Fillbarrell | Porters Perfection | |

## LITTLE-KNOWN WORKS BY POPULAR AUTHORS

John Buchan, *The Law Relating to the Taxation of Foreign Income*

J. R. R. Tolkien, *A Middle English Vocabulary*

T. S. Eliot, *The Classics and the Man of Letters*

Roald Dahl, *You Only Live Twice* (screenplay)

Winston Churchill, *Savrola* (novel)

George Eliot (Mary Ann, later Marian, Evans), *Feuerbach's Essence of Christianity* (translation)

Evelyn Waugh, *Rossetti* (biography)

John Le Carré (David Cornwell), *A Murder of Quality* (crime novel)

Sir Walter Ralegh, *Report of the Truth of the Fight about the Iles of Açores*

Jane Austen, *Lady Susan*

---

## PROMINENT BASILS

Brush
Hume
plant
Liddell Hart
Fawlty
d'Oliveira
the Great, Saint
I, of Macedon
II, Bulgaroctonus
'The Pot of' (Keats)
and tomato salad

## WARS WITH STUPID NAMES

of Jenkins's Ear
of the Roses
of 1812 (in fact, 1812–14)
Hundred Years
    (1337–1453 = 116 years)
Third Silesian
Yom Kippur
of Northern Aggression
against Terrorism
Servile
Cold

## SOME TITLES OF BOOKS AND PLAYS FEATURING NUMBERS

*The Thirty-Nine Steps*
*Fahrenheit 451*
*Mila 44*
*The Secret Seven mysteries*
*The Seven Pillars of Wisdom*
*Snow White and the Seven Dwarves*

*Catch-22*
*Bravo Two Zero*
*The Famous Five mysteries*
*The Three Musketeers*
*The Forty-Ninth Parallel*
*When Eight Bells Toll*

---

## FILMS BY NUMBERS

10
Seven Brides for Seven Brothers
Three Faces of Eve
FBI Code 98
First Blood
Five Easy Pieces
The Four Seasons
The Four Feathers
42nd Street
The Magnificent Seven
55 Days at Peking
Fifty Million Frenchmen
Fifth Avenue Girl
52 Pick-up
Friday the 13th
The Seven Samurai
Nine to Five
Nine and a Half Weeks
9/30/55
1984
92 in the Shade
711 Ocean Drive
The Seven-Year Itch
1776

The Seventh Veil
Police Academy 1, 2, 3, 4, 5 and 6
84 Charing Cross Road
Ten Rillington Place
The Thing with Two Heads
A Thousand and One Nights
Three Sisters
Twelve Angry Men
Two Mules for Sister Sara
Airport 1975
Taking of Pelham 123
1941
1492
$8^1/_2$
The Inn of the Sixth Happiness
Ocean's Eleven
None But the Brave
Fashions of 1934
Abroad with Two Yanks
Across 110th Street
Convict 99
A Zed and Two Noughts
Zero Hour!
One of Our Aircraft is Missing

## SOME USEFUL SPELLS TO SEND BY TEXT MESSAGE

**DiBL DaBL DoBL**
**Mak Ya Bum Nt WoBL**
Dibble dabble dobble
Make your bum not wobble

**BI T Sprts of Bog & Mrsh**
**MA U GAn A FIn Mstash**
By the spirits of bog and marsh,
May you gain a fine moustache

**I of NUt & TO of Frg**
**HOmwrks Etn BI A Dog**
Eye of newt and toe of frog,
Homework's eaten by a dog!

**Mi Cldrn Hlds A POshn Strng**
**4U IL Wer MI LkE Thng**
My cauldron holds a potion strong
For you I'll wear my lucky thong!

**W/ Ths SpeL T Ansas ClEr**
**Cum & join Me 4 A BEr**
With this spell the answer's clear
Come and join me for a beer!

**UR A Frt Ltl Mrt Dsinhrt**
You're a ferret. Little merit.
Disinherit!

---

## RODENT'S REVIEW

*The Mouse at Pooh Corner*
*Bleak Mouse*
*The Mouse on the Strand*
*The Mouse That Jack Built*
*Mouse Calls*
*Mouse of the Rising Sun*
*Mouses of the Holy*
*Mouseboat*
*The Mouse of Seven Gables*

*Mouse of Wax*
*Mousesitter*
*The Mouse That Dripped Blood*
*The Fall of the Mouse of Usher*
*A Mouse Is Not a Home*
*A Mouse For Mr Biswas*
*Mouse and Garden*
*Mouse Beautiful*
*The Three Mouseketeers*

---

## DOG OPERAS

Corgi and Bess
The Flying Dachshund
Dog Giovanni
Fidolio
Le Nozze de Fido
Die Fledermutt

Fido and Aeneas
Eugene Bonegin
Joan of Bark (Verdi)
I Pugliacci
Richard Cur de Lion
The Tails of Hoffman

## WELL-KNOWN NAMES THAT CHANGED

1. Marathon became Snickers (confectionery)

2. Oil of Ulay became Oil of Olay (moisturizers)

3. Lord Carrington (two 'r's) became Baron Carington (one 'r') (British politician)

4. Prince became ⚥ (pop star)

5. Hepworth's became Next (clothes retailer)

6. Opal Fruits became Starburst (confectionery)

7. Jif became Cif (household cleaner)

8. Channel Five became Five (TV station)

9. Channel Five Video became Polygram Video (prerecorded-video manufacturer)

10. French fries became Freedom fries (US potato chips)

11. Midland Bank became HSBC (financial institution)

12. St Petersburg became Petrograd became St Petersburg (Soviet/Russian city)

13. Rhodesia became Zimbabwe (African state)

14. Finisterre became Fitzroy (causing great sadness among avid listeners to the BBC's shipping forecast)

---

## STUPID AMERICAN PRESIDENTS

1. George W. Bush

## SOME PARTS OF A SHIP OR BOAT

after deck
anchor
berth
bilge
bilge keel
bitt
board
boat deck
bow
brig
bull's-eye
carline
chain locker
chart room
companionway
crow's nest
daggerboard
davit
engine room

false keel
figurehead
fo'c'sle
gangway
glory hole
guard rail
half-deck
hatchway
hawser
keel
larboard
lazaretto
mainmast
maintop
mizzen mast
mizzentop
monkey rail
orlop deck
outrigger

pilot house
pintle
Plimsoll line
poop
porthole
promenade deck
propeller shaft
prow
radio room
riding lamp
rigger
rowlock
rudder
scupper
skeg
spanker
stabilizer

---

## SKIPPING RHYME

Nebuchadnezzar, King of the Jews,
Bought his wife a pair of shoes
When the shoes began to wear
Nebuchadnezzar began to swear
When the swear began to stop
Nebuchadnezzar bought a shop
When the shop began to sell
Nebuchadnezzar bought a bell
When the bell began to ring
Nebuchadnezzar began to sing
Do re me fa so la ti do

## SOME COMMON ABBREVIATIONS FOR TXT MSGS

1. FTC? – (are you) free to chat?
2. IMHO – in my humble opinion
3. AFAIK – as far as I know
4. OTT – over the top
5. L8r – (see you) later
6. CU – see you
7. WAN2TLK? – do you want to talk?
8. ASAP – as soon as possible
9. BCNU – be seeing you
10. B4 – before
11. BB4N – bye-bye for now
12. Gr8 – great
13. HAND – have a nice day
14. Hot4U – hot for you
15. KIT – keep in touch
16. NE – any
17. Ti2GO – time to go
18. X – kiss
19. xoxoxoxo – hugs and kisses
20. YYSSW – yeah, yeah, sure, sure, whatever

---

## TOP NINE INTERNET SCAMS

The US Federal Trade Commission recently carried out a year-long law-enforcement effort targeting the top ten Internet scams, culling information from five US agencies, consumer-protection organizations from 9 countries and 23 states, and found 251 law-enforcement actions against online scammers in 'Operation Top Ten Dot Cons'. The top 10 scams were culled from Consumer Sentinel, a database of more than 285,000 consumer complaints established and maintained by the Federal Trade Commission.

1. scams by internet service providers (ISPs)
2. scams concerning Internet website design/promotions
3. scams concerning Internet information and adult services, requiring use of credit cards
4. scams concerning multilevel marketing/pyramid selling
5. scams concerning business opportunities and working from home
6. investment schemes and get-rich-quick scams
7. travel/vacation fraud
8. telephone/pay-per-call solicitation frauds (including modem diallers and videotext)
9. healthcare frauds

**HOW TO MISS AN ANIMAL**

1 Shoot *over* an animal running from you.

2 Shoot *under* one coming towards you.

3 Shoot *in front* of one crossing you.

## NAMES OF POP GROUPS

Dickie Do and the Don'ts

Dave Dee, Dozy, Beaky, Mick and Titch

The 'The'

Kilburn and the High Roads

## SOME FASCINATING GRAMMATICAL AND LINGUISTIC TERMS

**appellative:** common noun used as a name (Mother, Doctor)

**appositive:** of or pertaining to apposition, where the phrase means both its words or elements (drummer boy, oak tree, manservant)

**cataphora:** use of a pronoun ('this', 'him', 'its') to refer to something that hasn't been said yet: 'I want to say this: be home by twelve o'clock, or else.'

**diachronic:** concerned with the historical development of a language.

**extralinguistic:** elements beyond the words uttered, such as body language or prior knowledge that makes the words make sense (knowing, for instance, who 'he' is or where 'there' is).

**fronting:** unusual placing of a sentence element at the beginning of the sentence ('This I cannot stand!').

**greengrocer's apostrophe:** unnecessary apostrophe in an ordinary plural, so called because examples of it are to be found in greengrocery shops advertising 'pea's – half price' or 'cabbage's at 80 pence a pound'.

**hybrid:** word formed from words or elements from different languages, usually with the use of prefixes ('anti-', 'non-') or suffixes ('-ive', '-ist'), most of which are of Latin or Greek origin but sit well with Old English words.

**indirect speech:** also called 'reported speech', this is a way of reporting what someone said without using direct quotations ('She said the van would call today.')

**jussive:** indicating a command ('Behave'; 'Listen up, everybody').

**kernel clause:** sometimes called a 'kernel sentence', it is a basic sentence form that's had nothing done to it (it's not in the negative, not been made passive, not 'transformed' in any other way), and is complete in itself.

**level:** any of the areas in which a language can be analysed – for its meaning, sound or function, for instance.

**main clause:** a clause that is not subordinate to any other in the sentence.

**nominal:** functioning like a noun, even if not normally a noun ('the great and the good').

**orthography:** study of how words are spelled.

**palato-alveolar:** sound made by the action of the tongue on both the hard palate and the alveolar ridge (which is just behind the top front teeth) – for instance, the 'ch' sound in 'church'.

**quantifier:** something that determines number or amount ('many', 'much', 'several').

**Received Pronunciation:** often called 'RP', the 'Queen's English', 'BBC English', 'standard English', the south-influenced speech of what are regarded as educated people.

**second person:** the person addressed ('you'), 'I' and 'we' being the first person and 'he', 'she' and 'they' being the third person.

**triphthong:** vowel sound containing three distinct elements: 'hour', for instance, has the vowel elements 'a', a short 'oo' and the neutral vowel that says 'er'.

**umlaut:** a diacritic mark above a letter to indicate a mutation, especially in German.

**verb:** word in a sentence that defines the 'doing' of something. In 'She cut the grass', 'cut' is the verb.

**weak vowel:** the neutral vowel or vowel sound in a word that is not given its full value, such as the third vowel sound in 'miscellany'.

**yes-no question:** one that is capable of being answered with a straight 'yes' or 'no'. The verb is usually put before the subject, as in 'Will he come?'; 'Is this the one?'; 'Have you been there?'

**zero that-clause:** a clause from which 'that' is absent ('I said it would rain' instead of 'I said that it would rain.'

---

## EXTINCT SCOTCH AND IRISH CLANS

MacWesolowski
O'Bernstein
O'Dinga of O'Dinga
M'Dear
O'Press
McGhali of Boutros of That Ilk
MacHine
MacAbre
O'Dear
MacRamé
von Stumm

## WORDS TO BE AVOIDED IN GENTEEL CONVERSATION

throb
moist
spasm
clench
lick
lubricate
thrust
spend
penetrate
climax
rub

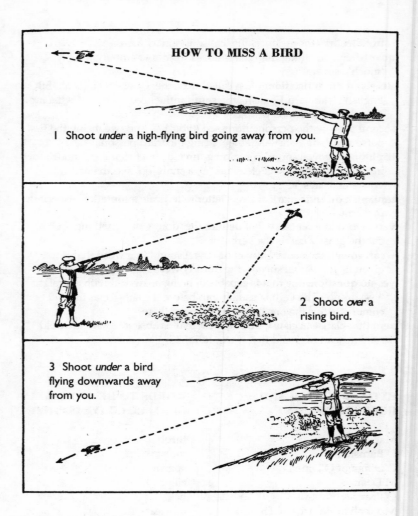

**HOW TO MISS A BIRD**

1 Shoot *under* a high-flying bird going away from you.

2 Shoot *over* a rising bird.

3 Shoot *under* a bird flying downwards away from you.

## SHAPES OF LENSES

| | |
|---|---|
| biconcave | convex |
| biconvex | planoconcave |
| concave | planoconvex |

## THINGS TO SAY VERY LOUDLY FROM THE STALLS DURING THEATRICAL PERFORMANCES

'Good God! Is this really *King Lear*? I thought it was *The Caretaker* . . . '

'Awful common way of speaking!'

'How much longer till the interval?'

'TAKE YOUR HAND OFF MY THIGH!'

'I must say, she's much smaller in the flesh, and her skin's awful . . . '

'Really, Fo is so *vieux jeu*'

'I can't wait to see the reviews to find out whether I enjoyed this or not'

'Hello? . . . Yes, I'm in the theatre . . . No, it's all right – it doesn't ring that loudly . . . '

'For God's sake, man, stop mumbling your lines!'

'Of course, if you'd seen Schofield's Hamlet, you'd know what a waste of time this is'

---

## DEGREES OF SLIMINESS (THE 'BRAGG SCALE')

1. sloppy
2. pulpy
3. sludgy
4. gelatinous
5. colloid
6. semiliquid
7. viscid
8. oozing
9. phlegmy
10. mucous

## RARELY USED MURDER WEAPONS

Flymo
smoked trout
Magimix
Coca-Cola®
grass
Lego™
paper underwear
soup spoon
vinyl LP
first-class stamp

## A CHEAT'S GUIDE TO LITERATURE
*Most literary conversations can be successfully managed even if you have not read the books by using these lines judiciously.*

**Lord of the Flies** – *William Golding*
FIRST LINES: The boy with fair hair lowered himself down the last few feet of rock and began to pick his way towards the lagoon.
LAST WORDS: He turned away to give them time to pull themselves together; and waited, allowing his eyes to rest on the trim cruiser in the distance.

**Hard Times** – *Charles Dickens*
FIRST LINES: 'Now, what I want is, Facts.'
LAST WORDS: We shall sit with lighter bosoms on the hearth, to see the ashes of our fires turn gray and cold.

**Mrs Dalloway** – *Virginia Woolf*
FIRST LINES: Mrs Dalloway said she would buy the flowers herself.
LAST WORDS: For there she was.

**A Passage to India** – *E. M. Forster*
FIRST LINES: Except for the Marabar Caves – and they are twenty miles off – the city of Chandrapore presents nothing extraordinary.
LAST WORDS: But the horses didn't want it – they swerved apart; the earth didn't want it, sending up rocks through which riders must pass single-file; the temples, the tank, the jail, the palace, the birds, the carrion, the Guest House, that came into view as they issued from the gap and saw Mau beneath: they didn't want it, they said in their hundred voices, 'No, not yet,' and the sky said, 'No, not there.'

**20,000 Leagues Under the Sea** – *Jules Verne*
FIRST LINES: In the year 1866 the whole maritime population of Europe and America was excited by an inexplicable phenomenon.
LAST WORDS: These two men are Captain Nemo and I.

**Lady Chatterley's Lover** – *D. H. Lawrence*
FIRST LINES: Ours is essentially a tragic age, so we refuse to take it tragically.
LAST WORDS: John Thomas says good-night to Lady Jane, a little droopingly, but with a hopeful heart.

**Three Men in a Boat** – *Jerome K. Jerome*
FIRST LINES: There were four of us – George, and William Samuel Harris, and myself, and Montmorency.
LAST WORDS: And Montmorency, standing on his hind legs, before the window, peering out into the night, gave a short bark of decided concurrence with the toast.

**Far From the Madding Crowd** – *Thomas Hardy*
FIRST LINES: When Farmer Oak smiled, the corners of his mouth spread till they were within an unimportant distance of his ears, his eyes were reduced to chinks, and diverging wrinkles appeared round them, extending upon his countenance like the rays in a rudimentary sketch of the rising sun.
LAST WORDS: 'But since 'tis as 'tis, why, it might have been worse, and I feel my thanks accordingly.'

**Moby-Dick** – *Herman Melville*
FIRST LINES: 'Call me Ishmael.'
LAST WORDS: It was the devious-cruising Rachel, that in her retracing search after her missing children, only found another orphan.

**Of Mice and Men** – *John Steinbeck*
FIRST LINES: A few miles south of Soledad, the Salinas River drops in close to the hill-side bank and runs deep and green.
LAST WORDS: And Carlson said: 'Now what the hell ya suppose is eatin' them two guys?'

**Jane Eyre** – *Charlotte Brontë*
FIRST LINES: There was no possibility of taking a walk that day.
LAST WORDS: 'Daily He announces more distinctly, "Surely I come quickly!" and hourly I more eagerly respond, "Amen; even so, come, Lord Jesus!"'

**Gulliver's Travels** – *Jonathan Swift*
FIRST LINES: My father had a small estate in Nottinghamshire; I was the third of five sons.
LAST WORDS: I dwell the longer upon this subject, from the desire I have to make the society of an English Yahoo, by any means, not insupportable; and, therefore, I here entreat those who have any tincture of this absurd vice, that they will not presume to come in my sight.

**A Portrait of the Artist as a Young Man** – *James Joyce*
FIRST LINES: Once upon a time and a very good time it was there was a moocow coming down along the road and this moocow that was coming down along the road met a nicens little boy named baby tuckoo. . .
LAST WORDS: Old father, old artificer, stand me now and ever in good stead.

**The Hobbit** – *J. R. R. Tolkien*
FIRST LINES: In a hole in the ground there lived a hobbit.
LAST WORDS: 'Thank goodness!' said Bilbo laughing, and handed him the tobacco-jar.

**Brave New World** – *Aldous Huxley*
FIRST LINES: A squat grey building of only thirty-four stories.
LAST WORDS: South-south-west, south, south-east, east . . .

**The Mill on the Floss** – *George Eliot*
FIRST LINES: A wide plain, where the broadening Floss hurries on between its green banks to the sea, and the loving tide, rushing to meet it, checks its passage with an impetuous embrace.
LAST WORDS: The tomb bore the names of Tom and Maggie Tulliver, and below the names it was written – 'In their death they were not divided.'

**The Vicar of Wakefield** – *Oliver Goldsmith*
FIRST LINES: I was ever of opinion, that the honest man who married and brought up a large family, did more service than he who continued single and only talked of population.
LAST WORDS: It now only remained that my gratitude in good fortune should exceed my former submission in adversity.

**Kipps** – *H. G. Wells*
FIRST LINES: Until he was nearly arrived at manhood, it did not become clear to Kipps how it was that he had come into the care of an aunt and uncle instead of having a father and mother like other little boys.
LAST WORDS: 'Oo! – I dunno,' he said at last, and roused himself to pull.

**Company** – *Samuel Beckett*
FIRST LINES: A voice comes to one in the dark.
LAST WORDS: Alone.

**Dr Jekyll and Mr Hyde** – *Robert Louis Stevenson*
FIRST LINES: Mr Utterson the lawyer was a man of a rugged countenance, that was never lighted by a smile; cold, scanty and embarrassed in discourse; backward in sentiment; lean, long, dusty, dreary, and yet somehow lovable.
LAST WORDS: Here, then, as I lay down the pen, and proceed to seal up my confession, I bring the life of that unhappy Henry Jekyll to an end.

**The Woman in White** – *Wilkie Collins*
FIRST LINES: This is the story of what a Woman's patience can endure, and of what a Man's resolution can achieve.
LAST WORDS: Marian was the good angel of our lives – let Marian end our Story.

**The Heart of the Matter** – *Graham Greene*
FIRST LINES: Wilson sat on the balcony of the Bedford Hotel with his bald pink knees thrust against the ironwork.
LAST WORDS: 'And you may be in the right of it there, too,' Father Rank replied.

**Herzog** – *Saul Bellow*
FIRST LINES: If I am out of my mind, it's all right with me, thought Moses Herzog.
LAST WORDS: Not a single word.

**Le Morte D'Arthur** – *Sir Thomas Malory*
FIRST LINES: It befell in the days of the noble Uther Pendragon, when he was King of England, and so reigned, there was a mighty and a noble duke in Cornwall, that held long time war against him; and the duke was named the Duke of Tintagil.
LAST WORDS: 'Sir,' said he, 'I had it of Queen Morgan le Fay, sister unto King Arthur.'

**The Adventures of Tom Sawyer** – *Mark Twain*
FIRST LINES: 'Tom!' No answer.
LAST WORDS: Some day it may seem worth while to take up the story of the younger ones again, and see what sort of men and women they turned out to be; therefore it will be wisest not to reveal any of that part of their lives at present.

**Pride and Prejudice** – *Jane Austen*
FIRST LINES: It is a truth universally acknowledged, that a single man in possession of a good fortune, must be in want of a wife.
LAST WORDS: Darcy, as well as Elizabeth, really loved them; and they were both ever sensible of the warmest gratitude towards the persons who, by bringing her into Derbyshire, had been the means of uniting them.

**The Thirty-Nine Steps** – *John Buchan*
FIRST LINES: I returned from the City about three o'clock on that May afternoon pretty well disgusted with life.
LAST WORDS: But I had done my best service, I think, before I put on khaki.

**Little Women** – *Louisa M. Alcott*
FIRST LINES: 'Christmas won't be Christmas without any presents,' grumbled Jo, lying on the rug.
LAST WORDS: Whether it ever rises again, depends upon the reception given to the first act of the domestic drama, called 'LITTLE WOMEN'.

**The Pilgrim's Progress (Part One)** – *John Bunyan*
FIRST LINES: As I walked through the wilderness of this world, I lighted on a certain place, where was a den; and I laid me down in that place to sleep: and as I slept I dreamed a dream.
LAST WORDS: So I awoke, and behold it was a dream.

**Wuthering Heights** – *Emily Brontë*
FIRST LINES: I have just returned from a visit to my landlord – the solitary neighbour that I shall be troubled with.
LAST WORDS: I lingered round them, under that benign sky; watched the moths fluttering among the heath and harebells, listened to the soft wind breathing through the grass, and wondered how any one could ever imagine unquiet slumbers for the sleepers in that quiet earth.

**The Great Gatsby** – *F. Scott Fitzgerald*
FIRST LINES: In my younger and more vulnerable years my father gave me some advice that I've been turning over in my mind ever since.
LAST WORDS: So we beat on, boats against the current, borne back ceaselessly into the past.

**Tom Jones** – *Henry Fielding*
FIRST LINES: An author ought to consider himself not as a gentleman who gives a private or eleemosynary treat, but rather as one who keeps a public ordinary at which all persons are welcome for their money.
LAST WORDS: And such is their condescension, their indulgence, and their beneficence to those below them that there is not a neighbour, a tenant, or a servant who doth not most gratefully bless the day when Mr Jones was married to his Sophia.

**The Turn of the Screw** – *Henry James*
FIRST LINES: The story had held us, round the fire, sufficiently breathless, but except the obvious remark that it was gruesome, as, on Christmas eve in an old house, a strange tale should essentially be, I remember no comment uttered till somebody happened to say that it was the only case he had met in which such a visitation had fallen on a child.
LAST WORDS: We were alone with the quiet day, and his little heart, dispossessed, had stopped.

**The Diary of a Nobody** – *George and Weedon Grossmith*
FIRST LINES: My dear wife Carrie and I have just been a week in our new house, 'The Laurels', Brickfield Terrace, Holloway – a nice six-roomed residence, not counting basement, with a front breakfast-parlour.
LAST WORDS: 'With much love to all, from The same old Lupin.'

**To Kill a Mockingbird** – *Harper Lee*
FIRST LINES: When he was nearly thirteen my brother Jem got his arm badly broken at the elbow.
LAST WORDS: He would be there all night, and he would be there when Jem waked up in the morning.

**The Trial** – *Franz Kafka*
FIRST LINES: Somebody must have made a false accusation against Josef K., for he was arrested one morning without having done anything wrong.
LAST WORDS: It was as if the shame would outlive him.

**Nineteen Eighty-Four** – *George Orwell*
FIRST LINES: It was a bright cold day in April, and the clocks were striking thirteen.
LAST WORDS: He loved Big Brother.

**Jamaica Inn** – *Daphne du Maurier*
FIRST LINES: It was a cold grey day in late November.
LAST WORDS: He laughed then, and took her hand, and gave her the reins; and she did not look back over her shoulder again, but set her face towards the Tamar.

**The Catcher in the Rye** – *J. D. Salinger*
FIRST LINES: If you really want to hear about it, the first thing you'll probably want to know is where I was born, and what my lousy childhood was like, and how my parents were occupied and all before they had me, and all that David Copperfield kind of crap, but I don't feel like going into it, if you want to know the truth.
LAST WORDS: If you do, you start missing everybody.

**Dracula** – *Bram Stoker*
FIRST LINES: Left Munich at 8.35 p.m. on 1st May, arriving at Vienna early next morning; should have arrived at 6.46, but train was an hour late.
LAST WORDS: 'Already he knows her sweetness and loving care; later on he will understand how some men so loved her, that they did dare much for her sake.'

**Decline and Fall** – *Evelyn Waugh*
FIRST LINES: Mr Sniggs, the Junior Dean, and Mr Postlethwaite, the Domestic Bursar, sat alone in Mr Sniggs's room overlooking the garden quad at Scone College.
LAST WORDS: Then he turned out the light and went into his bedroom to sleep.

---

## SOME WAYS TO EAT EGGS

boiled
scrambled
coddled
poached
fried
benedict
florentine

## SOME WAYS TO TIE HAIR

bun
plaits
braids
dreadlocks
bunches
ponytail
French plait

## HOUSEHOLD PESTS

silverfish   moth   ant   flea   cockroach

---

## HEALTH MATTERS

A man named Charles Osborne had the hiccups for approximately sixty-nine years

A blink lasts approximately 0.3 seconds

A sneeze can travel as fast as 100 miles per hour

A person will burn 7 per cent more calories if they walk on hard dirt compared to pavement

A yawn usually lasts for approximately six seconds

All babies are colour blind when they are born

Babies' eyes do not produce tears until the baby is approximately six to eight weeks old

During a typical human life span, the human heart will beat approximately 2.5 billion times

Enamel is the hardest substance in the human body

From the age of thirty, humans gradually begin to shrink in size

Girls have more tastebuds than boys

In a lifetime, an average human produces 10,000 gallons of saliva

Most heart attacks occur between the hours of 8am and 9am

On average, a person has 2 million sweat glands

## WAYS OF ESCAPING ATTACKS FROM WILD ANIMALS (PROBABLY)

**Attack from an unfriendly lion:**
Wait until the lion is five feet away and then ram a large pair of step ladders down its throat. If you cannot locate any step ladders in the jungle, then a small item of furniture such as a bedside table or a cocktail cabinet will do.

**Charge by an enraged bull:**
Bulls have notoriously weak bladders, so make the sound of running water, or begin to urinate yourself, and the bull will stop dead to take a leak.

**Crocodile attack:**
Look it straight in the eye, then stick out your tongue to touch the tip of your nose. A crocodile cannot stick out its tongue but it will be so impressed that it will try to copy you, causing its tongue to snap off. Then it will bleed to death.

**Seized by a gorilla:**
Go very limp and start to make little purring noises. The gorilla will think you are a female gorilla. He will roll you over and have rough sex with you after which he will fall asleep, allowing you to make his breakfast and then escape unscathed.

**Attack by a buzzard:**
Get a hobby! Buzzards are only attracted to dead meat.

**Elephant stampede:**
Blend seamlessly into the herd by putting your nose on your shoulder and waving your arm in front of you. The stampeding elephants will then run around you.

**Attack by a shark:**
Jam an oxygen cylinder into the shark's mouth, then fire at it with your last bullet.

**Attack by a shoal of piranhas:**
Get out of the water, asshole.

**Bear attack:**
Pretend to be a fish. The bear will bang your head against a rock to stun you. Then at least you won't feel anything when it rips both your arms off.

---

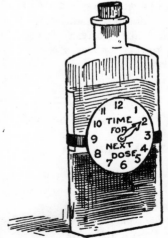

### DEVICES FOR JOGGING THE MEMORY

Papers put in front of clock or under watch case hardly escape notice.

## UNUSUAL/UNFORTUNATE PLACE NAMES IN BRITAIN

Trevor (Denbighshire, Wales)
Bottoms (West Yorkshire)
Spittal (Dyfed)
Little Snoring (Norfolk)
Muck (Inner Hebrides)
Loose (Kent)
Lover (Wiltshire)
Bogside (Glasgow & Derry)
Looe (Cornwall)
Messing (Essex)
Lower Assendon (Oxfordshire)
Portwrinkle (Cornwall)
Maggots End (Essex)
Pity Me (Durham)
Thong (Kent)
Sheepwash (Cornwall)
Twatt (Orkney)
Great Snoring (Norfolk)
Pratt's Bottom (Kent)
Slaggyford (Northumberland)
Knockin (Shropshire)
Wham (North Yorkshire)
Staylittle (Powys)
Swine (East Yorkshire)
Pale (Gwynedd)
Undy (Gwent)
Nether Wallop (Hampshire)

Nasty (Hertfordshire)
Skinflats (Central Scotland)
Bonkle (Lanarkshire)
Mid Yell (Shetland Isles)
Netherthong (West Yorkshire)
Windygates (Fife)
Petty (Grampians)
Tongue (Highlands)
Pant (Shropshire)
Nobottle (Northamptonshire)
Hole in the Wall (Herefordshire)
Grimness (Orkney Isles)
Rest and Be Thankful (Strathclyde)
Great Heck (North Yorkshire)
Pont-y-pant (Gwynedd)
Nitshill (Strathclyde)
Crackpot (North Yorkshire)
Lower Slaughter (Gloucestershire)
Dykehead (Strathclyde)
Ogle (Northumberland)
Gloup (Shetland Isles)
Killin (Central Scotland)
North Piddle (Worcestershire)
Gay Street (West Sussex)
Catbrain (Avon)
Pert (Tayside)

---

## AMERICAN PRESIDENTS WHO WERE NEVER ELECTED TO OFFICE

1. Gerald R. Ford, 1974–7 (also, never elected as vice-president, a post he held under President Richard Nixon from 1973 to 1974)
2. George W. Bush, 2001–present (presidency conferred upon him by a Supreme Court decision after disputed result in Florida)

## ELECTROMAGNETIC WAVES

| | |
|---|---|
| gamma rays | radio waves |
| infrared radiation | submillimetre radiation |
| light | ultraviolet radiation |
| microwaves | visible radiation |
| radar waves | X-rays |

---

## INTERESTING THINGS ABOUT NEW ZEALAND

contains more bookshops and golf courses per capita than any other country

has more sheep per capita than any other country in the world. In 1997, the sheep numbered about 47.4 million

the first country in the world to see the sunrise

boasts the most southerly railway station, vineyard, pub and national capital (Wellington) in the world

NZ's largest city, Auckland, hosts more boats per capita than any other city in the world

the capital, Wellington, boasts more restaurants per capita than even New York City

NZ is the most wired (with access to the Internet) nation on the face of the earth. Wellington, in particular, ranks number 1 as the most wired city in the world on a per-capita basis

has the second highest rate of car ownership in the world on a per-capita basis

New Zealand was also the first country in the world to:
give women the vote/adopt the eight-hour working day/operate a tourist board/introduce the retirement pension

## A GOOD WIFE'S GUIDE 1955

Prepare yourself for your husband's homecoming. Take fifteen minutes to rest so you will be refreshed when he arrives. Retouch your make-up, put a ribbon in your hair and be fresh looking. He has just been with a lot of work-weary people.

Be a little gay and a little more interesting for him. His boring day may need a lift and one of your duties is to provide it.

Listen to him. You may have a dozen important things to tell him, but the moment of his arrival is not the time.

Don't greet him with complaints and problems.

Don't complain if he's late for dinner or even if he stays out all night. Count this as minor compared to what he might have gone through that day.

Don't ask him questions about his actions or question his judgement or integrity. Remember, he is master of the house and as such will always exercise his will with fairness and truthfulness. You have no right to question him.

A good wife knows her place.

---

**POPULAR ENVELOPES**

windowed
plain brown
self-adhesive
padded
deckled
peel and seal
manilla
Armour pocket
Armour gusset pocket

**UNUSUAL SPORTSMEN'S NAMES**

Daniel Shittu (footballer)
John Bumstead (footballer)
Harvey Trump (cricketer)
Dean Windass (footballer)
Paul Dickov (footballer)
Nicky Butt (footballer)
Julian Dicks (footballer)
Doudou Mbombo (footballer)

## SILLY SAUSAGES

skinless wonder
sunburnt tomato
cummerband
pass the duchy
old banger
chilly dog
hentail
chippo latte
pork scratchings
pig Bertha

## MOVIES FEATURING TRANSPORT

*A Streetcar Named Desire*
*Shanghai Express*
*Airplane*
*The Ship of Fools*
*Showboat*
*Yellow Submarine*
*Murder on the Orient Express*
*Taxi Driver*

---

## CONTEMPORARY OPERAS

S. Berlusconi (lib. by C. Gent): *I Gatti Grassi* (*The Fatcats*); features the tenor arias 'Che gelida pensione' ('Your tiny pension is frozen') and 'O mio caro stipendio' ('O my beloved salary')

J.-C. Philipoussis (lib. by S. &. V. Williams): *La Fille de Wimbledon*; features the bass aria 'Renonce-toi a jouer, Timothé!' (Give up, Timothy!') and the chorus 'Tu ne peut jamais gagner!' ('You can never win!')

S.-G. Eriksson (lib. by V. Beckham): *Ariadne im Argos* (features the soprano/contralto duet 'Wo, wo ist der Katalog, Liebling?' ('Where, my darling, O where, is the catalogue?')

G. W. Bush & A. R. P. Blair (lib. by A. Campbell & D. Rumsfeld): *À La Recherche des Armes Perdus* (*In Search of Missing Weapons*); features the so-called 'Lying Chorus', 'Nous avons trouvés les armements d'anéantissement de masse', ('We have found the WMDs') and the tenor/baritone duet 'Va faire pipi, Be-be-se!' ('P**s off, BBC!')

D. Dolce & S. Gabbana (lib. by G. Orwell [E. A. Blair]): *Nella Casa di Fratello Grosso* (*In the House of Big Brother*); features the coloratura soprano aria 'O venerdi spaventosissimo!' ('O most terrible Friday!')

## SHORTEST PLACE NAMES IN BRITAIN

Nox (Shropshire)
Hoo (Suffolk)
Lee (Lancashire)
Par (Cornwall)
Ham (Highlands)
Ord (Isle of Skye)
Usk (Gwent)
How (Cumbria)
Hill (Bristol)
Mey (Highlands)
Kew (Greater London)
Old (Northamptonshire)
Wix (Essex)
Lye (Birmingham)
Row (Cumbria)
Hoe (Norfolk)
Esh (Durham)
Moy (Highlands)
Ose (Isle of Skye)
Lew (Oxfordshire)

Rhu (Dunbartonshire)
Esh (Durham)
Ide (Devon)
Ore (East Sussex)
Wem (Shropshire)
Ley (Cornwall)
Raw (North Yorkshire)
Uig (Highlands)
Rye (East Sussex)
Voe (Shetland)
Lea (Lincolnshire)
Ham (Kent)
Ash (Kent)
Wye (Kent)
Kea (Cornwall)
Ely (Cambridgeshire)
Lag (Dumfriesshire)
Law (Strathclyde)
Eye (Suffolk)

---

## SOME COMMON EMOTICONS

1. -! no
2. -!! definitely not
3. '" sour puss
4. %*@:-( I am hung over with a headache
5. %-6 not very clever
6. (:+( ooh, I'm scared
7. ((_0_)) fat arse
8. (((H))) a big hug
9. (:-& I am angry
10. (:-D blabbermouth
11. (:- I K- this is a formal message
12. (@ @) you're kidding
13. * you're a star
14. **-( I am very, very shocked
15. *:O) bozo
16. *G* giggle
17. :-( sad
18. :-) happy
19. :-))) very happy
20. *X* kiss

## SOME TRACTORS AND COMBINE HARVESTERS

| | | |
|---|---|---|
| New Holland | Claas | Massey Ferguson |
| Case International Harvester | John Deere | Deutz-Fahr |

---

### TOP GRAMMATICAL ERRORS ON BBC RADIO 4
*(You find them on all radio stations and in newspapers,
but Britain's flagship Radio 4 should know better!)*

1. try and ('try to')

2. choose between A or B ('A and B', since you can't choose between
one thing)

3. try and ('try to')

4. neither A or B ('nor')

5. each have their own ... (each has)

6. one of those people who is ('one of those people who are' – think,
'those people who are, one of'; 'those people', not 'one', is the clause
subject governing the verb 'to be'; lecture over)

7. neither he nor she are ('is')

8. the committee has submitted their report ('has submitted its' or
'have submitted their')

9. due to them being there ('their being there' – 'being' is a gerund,
works like a noun; it's the 'being', not the 'them', that it is due to;
sorry, no more lectures)

10. looking at the economy in the past quarter, the interest rate seems
to be... (the interest rate is not looking at anything – this is often
called a dangling or misrelated construction)

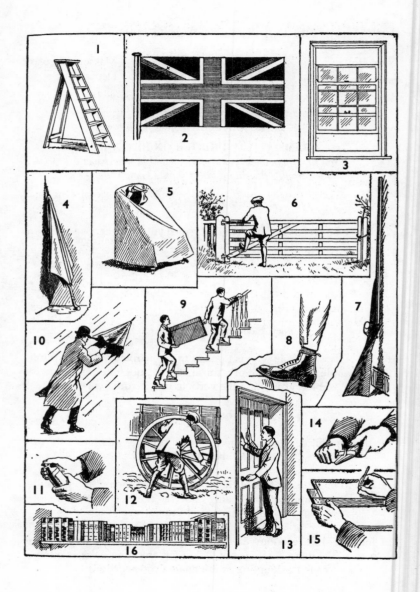

## THE RIGHT WAY OF DOING THINGS (SEE LEFT)

1.  Open a step ladder fully before mounting it.
2.  A Union Jack must have the broad white stripe of the diagonal cross (X) upwards near the pole.
3.  To ventilate a room, open the sash at the top as well as at the bottom.
4.  Stand a wet umbrella handle downwards to drain.
    This preserves the silk near the stick.
5.  Spread a wet cycle cape over a chair to dry.
6.  Get over a locked gate at the hinge end.
7.  Stand a gun or rifle with barrel vertical.
8.  Pull up your trousers to the top of your boots before putting on trouser clips. This prevents them bagging at the knees.
9.  How to carry a heavy box upstairs.
10. On a windy day face the wind to open an umbrella.
11. When opening a bottle of ink or other liquid that may damage your clothes turn the neck away from you.
12. How to help a stuck cart.
13. Push a jammed door at the point where it sticks.
14. When using a knife, make the strokes outwards, away from you.
15. When accurate ruling has to be done, place the pencil point on the exact point through which the line has to be drawn, and move the ruler or square up to it.
16. Put the heavier books at the ends of a shelf.

---

### MAXIMS FOR LIFE II

Fill your lungs well with air before blowing a soap bubble.

In motoring, high speed means high tyre costs.

Gloomy blue sky – wind; bright blue sky – good weather.

Tight and unventilated headgear produces baldness.

All debts should be regarded as debts of honour.

## WAR-COMIC EXPRESSIONS

'Donner und blitzen!'
'Achtung! Schpitfeuer!'
'Teufel!'
'For you, Tommy, zer var iss over'
'Keep firing, lads!'
'That's for Chalky, Fritz!'
'Aaaarrrrgggghhhh!'
'Good on you, Yank!'
'Gott in Himmel!'
'Cripes, sarge, they've got Dusty!'

## WAR-COMIC TERMS FOR ENEMY AND ALLIED SOLDIERS

Jerry, Fritz
Eyetie
Nip
Canuck
Yank
Digger
Kiwi
Frenchy

---

## TWENTY-ONE NOTABLE DEAD ENGINEERS

1. Edwin Armstrong (1890–1954) – American
2. John Logie Baird (1888–1945) – Briton
3. Sir Joseph Bazalgette (1819–91) – Briton
4. Sir Henry Bessemer (1813–98) – Briton
5. Wernher von Braun (1912–77) – German-born American
6. Sir Marc Isambard Kingdom Brunel (1769–1849) – French-born Briton
7. Lee De Forest (1873–1961) – American
8. Rudolf Diesel (1858–1913) – German
9. Anthony Fokker (1890–1939) – Dutch-born American
10. Sergei Ilyushin (1894–1977) – Russian
11. Hugo Junkers (1959–1935) – German
11. Guglielmo Marconi (1874–1937) – Italian
12. Henry Maudslay (1771–1831) – Briton
13 Thomas Newcomen (1663–1729) – Briton
14. Ferdinand Porsche (1875–1951) – Austrian
15. Thomas Savery (1650–1715) – Briton
16. Ernst Werner von Siemens (1816–92) – German
17. George Stephenson (1781–1848) – Briton
18. Thomas Telford (1757–1834) – Briton
19. Nikola Tesla (1856–1943) – American
20. James Watt (1736–1819) – Briton
21. Sir Frank Whittle (1907–96) – Briton

## TOILET-RELATED EUPHEMISMS

*The Toilet (n.)*

bog
boghouse
can
cloakroom
closet
comfort room
dunny
dyke
the Gents
Holy of Holies
jakes
jericho
john
kharzy
the Ladies
lav'
little boys' room
little girls' room
loo
necessary house
netty
place of easement
place of repose
powder room
privy
proverbial
rest room
retiring place
shady place
shit-house
smallest room
thinking place
throne
thunderbox
WC

*Go to the toilet (vb)*

answer the call of
  nature
be excused
check on the scones
do the necessary
ease yourself
explore the geography
  of the house
find a haven of refuge
freshen up
go into retreat
go to Egypt
go to the library
go to your private
  office
lay some cable
mail a letter
pay a visit to your
  uncle
pick a rose
powder your nose
relieve yourself
see a man about a
  horse
see your aunt
shoot a dog
shoot a lion
use the cloakroom
use the facilities
visit Sir John
visit the bathroom
visit the old soldiers'
  home
wash your hands

## TWENTY PAIRS OF GREAT LOVERS IN FICTION AND IN LIFE

1. Antony and Cleopatra
2. W. H. Auden and Christopher Isherwood
3. Bonnie and Clyde
4. Richard Burton and Elizabeth Taylor
5. Lord Byron and Lady Caroline Lamb
6. Lady Chatterley and Mellors
7. Daphnis and Chloë
8. Darby and Joan
9. Edward VIII and Wallis Simpson
10. Harlequin and Columbine
11. Heathcliff and Cathy
12. Jane Eyre and Edward Rochester
13. Anna Karenina and Alexei Vronski
14. Henry Miller and Anaïs Nin
15. Paris and Helen
16. Porgy and Bess
17. Rimbaud and Verlaine
18. Tristan and Isolde
19. Oscar Wilde and Lord Alfred Douglas (Bosie)
20. Virginia Woolf and Vita Sackville-West

---

## RARE OR CURIOUS NAMES FOR PUBLIC HOUSES

The Average Ayatollah
The ISBN
Sebastian's Little Hole
Closed
The Jolly Peshmerga
The Hair-do
Bar Food No Overalls or Boots
The Amputee's Stump
The Watered Pint
Large-screen Sky Sports Live
   Karaoke Tuesdays

## CORNISH PLACE NAMES

Tremendous
Polpot
Penandink
Trepanning
Polyputthekettleon
Penultimate
Polygon
Pentagon
Tremolo
Polyzoan
Penumbra

## SOME LEADING DEAD FILM DIRECTORS

Frank Capra (1897–1991)
Richard Brooks (1912–92)
John Cassavetes (1929–89)
René Clair (1898–1981)
Jean Cocteau (1889–1963)
George Cukor (1899–1983)
Michael Curtiz (1888–1962)
Cecil B. De Mille (1881–1959)
Sergei Eisenstein (1898–1948)
Rainer Werner Fassbinder (1946–82)
Federico Fellini (1920–93)
John Ford (1895–1973)
D. W. Griffith (1875–1948)
Alfred Hitchcock (1899–1980)
John Huston (1906–87)
Stanley Kubrick (1928–99)
Fritz Lang (1890–1976)

David Lean (1908–91)
Sergio Leone (1921–89)
Joseph Losey (1909–84)
Joseph L. Mankiewicz (1909–93)
Vincente Minnelli (1910–86)
Pier Paolo Pasolini (1922–76)
Sam Peckinpah (1925–84)
Otto Preminger (1906–86)
Carol Reed (1906–76)
Roberto Rossellini (1906–77)
John Sturges (1911–92)
François Truffaut (1932–84)
King Vidor (1894–1982)
Luchino Visconti (1906–77)
Orson Welles (1915–85)
William Wyler (1902–81)
Fred Zinneman (1907–97)

---

## OBSCURE ROYAL APPOINTMENTS

Chief Paper Restorer, Royal Library
Yeoman of the Royal Pantries
Clerk of the Royal Kitchens
Royal Herbstrewer
Royal Goat Herd
Chief Binder, Royal Library
Bibliographer, Royal Library
Keeper of the Royal Philatelic
    Collection
Master of the Horse
Royal Swan Keeper
Royal Trustee
Queen's Bargemaster
Royal Waterman

Queen's Champion
Captain of the Queen's Flight
Queen's Piper
Queen's Remembrancer
Master of the Royal Badgers
Cakebaker Royal
Under Hamsterkeeper
Mistress of the Sofabed
Toastmaker-General
Master of the Queen's
    Wristwatch
Under-Hinter General
Officer of the Royal Innuendo
HM Chief Tabloid Lamenter

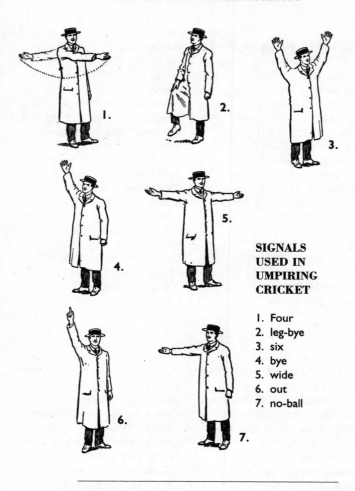

**SIGNALS
USED IN
UMPIRING
CRICKET**

1. Four
2. leg-bye
3. six
4. bye
5. wide
6. out
7. no-ball

---

## THE SEVEN WONDERS OF THE ISLE OF WIGHT

*Lake* you can walk through without wetting your feet
*Newtown* which is very old
*Newport* you cannot bottle
*Freshwater* you cannot drink

*Ryde* where you walk
*Needles* you cannot thread
*Cowes* you cannot milk

## SCOTCH PLACE NAMES

Auldschultye
Dunthat
Blair Aufoll
Water o' Minrall
Loch Tyte
Padloch
Gaimerbridge
Sound o' Sighlands
Tigh-t-na-Duchsass
Knockindhu
Inversuip

## FRENCH AVIATION TERMS USED IN ENGLISH

fuselage
longeron
aileron
aerodrome
balloon
aeroplane
roundel
dirigible
chandelle
parachute
aeronautics

---

## 'BUM' WORDS

1. bum – the buttocks; a habitual loafer or tramp; a lazy, dissolute person
2. bumboy – a young male homosexual (term of abuse)
3. bum rap – imprisonment on jumped-up charges (North American)
4. bum rolls – padded rolls worn on the hips under women's dresses in the sixteenth and seventeenth centuries.
5. bum freezer – a short jacket
6. bum-bag – a small bag worn on a belt around the waist or hips, used for carrying money or small items (British)
7. bum-bailiff – a bailiff with the authority to collect debts and arrest debtors
8. bum steer – false information (North American)
9. bum-boat – originally a scavenger's boat removing refuse from ships; later used to describe a small boat that takes provisions to ships
10. bum fluff – light, downy hair on an adolescent's face
11. bum note – a wrong note in music
12. bumfodder – toilet paper
13. bum time – a bad time or event
14. bum-baily – see bum-bailiff
15. bumsucker – a toady

## TWELVE THINGS TO DO TO OBTAIN PRIVACY IN A RAILWAY CARRIAGE

beckon to passers-by from the window

impersonate the sound of Formula One racing cars very quietly

snuggle up to the person sitting next to you

say to the person in the next seat 'Wake me up if I drool on your jacket'

mutter darkly

test your neighbour's reflexes with a small hammer

recite 'The Highwayman' by Alfred Noyes

light a cooking fire

eat a banana-and-watercress sandwich

masticate

use nail scissors purchased for the purpose to cut paper dollies from the newspaper of the person opposite

sing a selection of songs from the shows

---

## TWELVE RARE BREEDS OF DOG

spoofhound
ottoman
Liberian whelkhound
flat-chested retriever
lakmé
Bavarian Käsehund

water pi-dog
Bulgarian rizla
chesterfield
Norfolk dullard
crustatian
Old English snaffler

## SOME BORING SCHOOLS AND THEORIES

**absolutism:** holds that there is an ultimate reality that reconciles all differences.

**atomism:** holds that the entire universe is composed of distinct and indivisible units (this school of thought was about during the time of the ancient Greeks, and is not to be confused with modern physics).

**critical realism:** theory that reality is tripartite: as well as the mental and physical aspects of reality there is a third one called essences.

**dualism:** dualists believe that the world comprises two radically independent and absolute elements, be that good and evil, matter and spirit or mind and body.

**humanism:** a system that puts human interest before unproven ideas such as gods (modern-day humanism is often synonymous with atheism or agnosticism, but there are humanists among religions).

**idealism:** holds that thought or an idea is the basis of either knowledge or existence; that things exist only as products of the mind (cf. solipsism).

**meliorism:** belief that the world is capable of improvement, and that humankind has the power to bring it about; it comes somewhere between optimism and pessimism.

**neutral monism:** the theory that reality is not physical and not spiritual, but can express itself as either.

**optimism:** theory that says the universe we know is the best of all possible universes (cf. pessimism).

**pessimism:** holds that the universe is the worst possible one and everything is doomed (cf. optimism).

**solipsism:** belief that the only thing one can be sure of is one's own existence, and that true knowledge of anything else is impossible (cf. idealism).

**theism:** belief in the concept of God as a hypothesis for the existence of the universe; belief in gods.

---

## ENGLISH COUNTIES BEGINNING WITH B OR S

Bedfordshire/Berkshire/Buckinghamshire/Shropshire/Somerset/ Staffordshire/Suffolk/Surrey/Sussex

## TWENTY-ONE THINGS A GENTLEMAN SHOULD NEVER DO

eat soup at luncheon
own a BMW
wear monograms on his clothing
go skiing
be a member of the Garrick Club
say 'Cheers!'
hold his knife like a pen
wear any jewellery (a signet ring, if ancient, is just permitted)
be unconsciously rude
call himself a gentleman
refer to games – e.g. soccer – as 'sport' or 'sports'
live in Surrey
keep a tankard in the lounge bar of his local pub
refer to morning dress as a 'morning suit'
or a dinner jacket as a 'dinner suit'
have more than one button at his coat cuff (and that must function as
    a button)
write to newspapers
call a boating coat a 'blazer'
wear shorts (other than when taking part in games; see above)
live within his means
gain a reputation for working hard

---

## DEGREES OF SYCOPHANCY (THE 'FAWSLEY SCALE')

1. subservience
2. slavishness
3. obseqiousness
4. submissiveness
5. cringing
6. crawling
7. fawning
8. bootlicking
9. bumsucking
10. toadying
11. ingratiating
12. creeping
13. flunkyism
14. lackeyism
15. grovelling
16. kowtowing

## SOME YUP'IK ESKIMO (CENTRAL ALASKAN ESKIMO) WORDS RELATING TO SNOW

*qanuk* 'snowflake'
*qanir-* 'to snow'
*qanunge-* 'to snow'
*qanugglir-* 'to snow'
*kaneq* 'frost'
*kaner-* 'be frosty / frost sth.'
*kanevvluk* 'fine snow / rain particles'
*kanevcir-* to get fine snow / rain particles
*natquik* 'drifting snow / etc.
*natqu(v)igte-* 'for snow / etc. to drift along ground'
*nevluk* 'clinging debris'
*nevlugte-* 'have clinging debris /...'lint / snow / dirt...'
*aniu* 'snow on ground'
*aniu-* 'get snow on ground'
*apun* 'snow on ground'
*qanikcaq* 'snow on ground'
*qanikcir-* 'get snow on ground'
*muruaneq* 'soft deep snow'
*qerretrar-* 'for snow to crust'
*nutaryuk* 'fresh snow'
*qanisqineq* 'snow floating on water'
*qengaruk* 'snow bank'
*utvak* 'snow carved in block'
*navcaq* 'snow cornice, snow [formation] about to collapse'
*navcite-* 'get caught in an avalanche'
*pirta* 'blizzard, snowstorm'
*pircir-* 'to blizzard'
*pirtuk* 'blizzard, snowstorm'
*cellallir-, cellarrlir-* 'to snow heavily'
*pir(e)t(e)pag-* 'to blizzard severely'
*pirrelvag-* 'to blizzard severely'

*Steven A. Jacobson*, Yup'ik Eskimo Dictionary, *Fairbanks (AK)*,
*Alaska Native Language Center, University of Alaska, 1984*

## CULINARY TERMS FOR POSERS

**AL DENTE** Describes food, usually pasta or vegetables, cooked to be slightly firm to the bite.

**ANTIPASTI** Italian word for appetizers.

**APERITIF** Pre-meal alcoholic drink, intended to stimulate the appetite.

**ASPIC** Savoury jelly used to decorate meat and fish dishes.

**AU GRATIN** Food that is cooked in a sauce and topped with breadcrumbs and/or grated cheese and then browned.

**BOUQUET GARNI** Small bunch of herbs sometimes tied in muslin and added to flavour food during cooking.

**BOURGUIGNON, -ONNE** In the style of Burgundy.

**CANAPÉ** Small appetizer.

**CASSOULET** French stew prepared with beans, meat, sausages and vegetables.

**CHASSEUR** French dish containing mushrooms, shallots and white wine.

**COMPOTE** Dessert dish of fresh or dried fruit cooked in syrup and served cold.

**CROUTON** Diced bread, fried or toasted, added to a bowl of soup as a garnish.

**DAUBE** Stew of braised meat or poultry and vegetables.

**EN CROÛTE** Food cooked in a crust of pastry.

**EN PAPILLOTE** Food wrapped during cooking, usually in paper or foil, and served wrapped.

**ENTRÉE** The third course, following the appetizer and fish courses (can also refer to main course).

**FRICASSÉE** Poultry or other white meat served in a white sauce made with cream and egg yolk.

**GELATIN** Setting agent, made from animal protein and available in powdered or sheet form.

**GHEE** Clarified butter.

**GIBLETS** Edible internal organs and trimmings of a bird.

**GOULASH** Hungarian stew of meat and vegetables flavoured with paprika.

**HORS D'OEUVRE** Appetizers.

**JARDINIÈRE** Dish garnished with vegetables.

**JULIENNE** Finely shredded food, usually cooked or raw vegetables.

**MARINIÈRE** Mussels or other seafood cooked in herbs and white wine.

**MEUNIÈRE** Food, usually fish, cooked with butter, parsley, lemon juice.
**NAVARIN** Lamb or mutton casserole with vegetables.
**NOISETTE** Round of meat cut from a fillet.
**OFFAL** Edible internal organs of animals and birds.
**PÂTÉ** Mixture of meats, poultry, fish, game or vegetables, seasoned and
    baked, and then served cold.
**PULSES** Dried seeds of legumes.
**RAGOUT** Meat and vegetable stew.
**ROUX** Mixture of cooked butter and flour used as a base for a sauce.
**STUFFING** Mixture of vegetables, rice, herbs or fruit, or a combination of
    these, usually seasoned and put in a joint of meat or poultry before cooking.
**SUET** Hard animal fat most often used in pastry-making and baking.
**TOURNEDOS** Round and thick slice of beef fillet.
**TRUFFLE** Subterranean fungus used sparingly in dishes as a garnish and
    for its pungent flavour.
**VINAIGRETTE** Mixture of oil and vinegar flavoured with seasoning
    and/or herbs, often used as a salad dressing.
**ZEST** Oily layer of coloured skin on a citrus fruit.

---

## *BLUE PETER* PRESENTERS

1.  Christopher Trace (1958–67)
2.  Leila Williams (1958–62)
3.  Anita West (1962)
4.  Valerie Singleton (1962–72)
5.  John Noakes (1965–78)
6.  Peter Purves (1967–78)
7.  Lesley Judd (1972–9)
8.  Simon Groom (1978–86)
9.  Christopher Wenner (1978–80)
10. Tina Heath (1979–80)
11. Sarah Greene (1980–3)
12. Peter Duncan
    (1980–4 and 1985–6)
13. Janet Ellis (1983–7)
14. Michael Sundin (1984–5)
15. Mark Curry (1986–9)
16. Caron Keating (1986–90)
17. Yvette Fielding (1987–92)
18. John Leslie (1989–94)
19. Diane-Louise Jordan (1990–6)
20. Anthea Turner (1992–4)
21. Tim Vincent (1993–7)
22. Stuart Miles (1994–9)
23. Katy Hill (1995–2000)
24. Romana D'Annunzio (1996–8)
25. Konnie Huq (1997–present)
26. Richard Bacon (1997–8)
27. Simon Thomas (1999–present)
28. Matt Baker (1999–present)
29. Liz Barker (2000–present)
30. Basil Brush (2003)

## COOKING METHODS AS SEEN ON TELEVISION

**BAKE** Cook in an oven using dry heat.

**BARBECUE** Cook outside over an open fire, usually made of charcoal.

**BASTE** Spoon cooking juices or fat over the dish in order to retain moisture in food during cooking.

**BLANCH** Treat with boiling water (food can be briefly boiled or the water poured over it), to remove the skin, lessen strong flavours, or preserve colour prior to freezing.

**BOIL** Cook food in a liquid at a temperature of 100°C (212°F).

**BRAISE** Brown food lightly in fat, and then cook it slowly in a covered pot in only a small amount of liquid.

**CASSEROLE** Cook slowly in an oven in a covered casserole.

**CHINE** Separate the backbone (chine) from the rib bones before cooking to make serving easier.

**CURE** To preserve food, usually meat, fish, or poultry, by drying, salting, or smoking.

**DEEP-FRY** To fry food at high temperatures in oil deep enough to cover it.

**DEVIL** Prepare food before cooking with hot seasoning or a hot sauce.

**FILLET** Remove the bones from fish or meat.

**FLAMBÉ** Set light to alcoholic spirit that has been poured over food, burning the alcohol but leaving the flavour of the spirit.

**FRY** Cook food in a small quantity of oil in a shallow frying pan.

**GLAZE** Give a glossy appearance to food by coating with a substance, such as egg or milk (on pastry) or sugar glaze (on fruit).

**GRATE** Shred food such as vegetables or cheese using a serrated-edged grater.

**GRILL** Cook food under a direct radiating heat.

**KNEAD** Work through ingredients, usually in a dough and often with the hands, to mix the ingredients evenly.

**MARINATE** Soak food in a mixture (marinade), before cooking, to tenderize it and add flavour.

**MINCE** Cut or chop food, especially meat, into small pieces before cooking.

**PARBOIL** Partially cook by boiling before finishing the process by a different method.

**POACH** Simmer gently in a liquid.

**REDUCE** Boil something rapidly, such as a sauce, to reduce its volume by evaporation and concentrate its flavour.

**SAUTÉ** Cook very quickly in hot oil or fat, turning continuously.

**SCORE** Cut marks into the surface of a food, usually meat, to help it cook.

**SEAR** Seal the surface of a piece of meat or fish by browning it lightly in hot fat before cooking.

**SIMMER** Cook in liquid kept at just below boiling point.

**STEAM** Cook food in the steam that rises from boiling water placed below it.

**STEW** Simmer food slowly immersed in liquid, often in a casserole.

**STIR-FRY** Fry quickly over a high temperature (often in a Chinese wok) and with a continual stirring motion.

**STRAIN** Separate liquid from solid elements by passing food through a colander or sieve.

**SWEAT** Cook food gently, usually in a little fat, until the juices are released.

---

## POINTS OF TABLE ETIQUETTE

Soup should be taken noiselessly from the side of the spoon and the plate tilted away from the diner. Asparagus is lifted with the fingers, or with tongs, and only the tip is eaten. Remove the leaves of a globe artichoke with your fingers, and eat as illustrated.

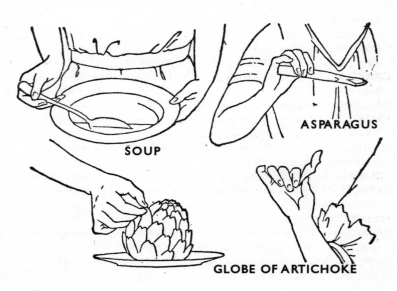

SOUP

ASPARAGUS

GLOBE OF ARTICHOKE

## PRIME NUMBERS WHOSE INDIVIDUAL DIGITS ADD UP TO...

| Ten | Eleven | Thirteen |
| --- | --- | --- |
| 37 | 29 | 67 |
| 109 | 47 | 139 |
| 163 | 83 | 157 |
| 181 | 137 | 193 |
| 271 | 191 | 283 |
| 307 | 263 | 337 |
| 433 | 227 | 409 |
| 523 | 281 | 463 |
| 541 | 317 | 607 |
| 613 | 353 | 643 |
| 631 | 443 | 661 |
| 811 | 461 | 733 |
| 1,009 | 641 | 823 |
| | 821 | |
| | 911 | |

---

## PERSONAL WEAPONS

| | | | |
| --- | --- | --- | --- |
| assegai | cosh | knife | sabre |
| axe | cudgel | knobkerrie | scimitar |
| battering ram | cutlass | knuckleduster | shillelagh |
| battleaxe | dagger | kris | skean-dhu |
| bayonet | dirk | kukri | staff |
| bilbo | épée | lance | stave |
| bill | falchion | lathi | stick |
| blade | flick knife | mace | stiletto |
| bludgeon | foil | machete | sword |
| bowie knife | gisarme | panga | swordstick |
| brass knuckles | halberd | parang | Toledo |
| broadsword | hanger | partisan | tomahawk |
| cavalry sword | harpoon | pike | truncheon |
| chopper | hatchet | poleaxe | yataghan |
| claymore | javelin | quarterstaff | |
| club | jerid | rapier | |

## BUFFYISMS

1. Hi, I'm Buffy … and you are history.
2. This is not gonna be pretty. We're talkin' violence, strong language, adult content.
3. That probably would've sounded more convincing if I wasn't wearing my Yummy Sushi pyjamas.
4. Can you vague that up for me?
5. WILLOW: Oh my God, Buffy!
   BUFFY: I know, they're gone. I guess we should chase them.
   WILLOW: No, your hair! It's adorable!
6. If the Apocalypse comes, beep me.
7. Now, we can do this the hard way, or … well, actually, there's just the hard way.
8. That much quality time with my mom would probably lead to some quality matricide.
9. Clark Kent has a job. I just want to go on a date.
10. To make you a vampire, they have to suck your blood, then you have to suck their blood. It's like a whole big sucking thing.
11. You're not like other boys at all. You are totally and completely one of the girls!
12. BUFFY: See, this is a school, and we have students, and they check out books, and then they learn things.
    GILES: I was beginning to suspect that was a myth.

---

## SOME INTRIGUING SURGICAL OPERATIONS

cheiloplasty: repair of lips
craniotomy: incision of skull
dermatoplasty: repair of skin
glossectomy: removal of all or part of tongue
orchidotomy: incision of testis
phalloplasty: repair of penis
polypectomy: removal of nasal polyps
polypnephrostomy: opening of kidney
rhinoplasty: repair of nose

## MEDICAL PROFESSIONALS' ABBREVIATIONS (THE ONES PATIENTS DON'T USUALLY SEE)

**AFAIAA** As far as I am aware
**ALSOB** Alcohol-like substance on breath
**AOB** Alcohol on breath
**BOGOF** Buy one, get one free
**BUNDY** But unfortunately not dead yet
**BWS** Beached-whale syndrome
**C₂H₅O +++** drunk (chemical formula for alcohol)
**CHAOS** Chief has arrived on scene
**CTD** Close to death / Circling the drain
**DFO** Done fell out
**DGF** Damned good f\*\*k (as allegedly prescribed for neurotic women)
**DIRTBAGS** Dirty indigent requesting transport because alcohol gives [him] seizures
**DRTTTT** Dead right there, there, there, and there (used after pedestrian/train altercations)
**FDGB** Fall down go boom
**FLK** Funny-looking kid
**FLM&D** Funny looking mum and dad
**FUBAR** F\*\*ked up beyond all recognition
**GOK** God only knows
**GOMA** Get out of my ambulance
**GOMER** Get out of my Emergency Room (US slang for an unwelcome patient)
**HSP** Heart-sink patient
**KISS** Keep it simple and stupid
**LASGLH** Lights and sirens, go like hell
**LOL** Little old lady
**MAGGOT** Medically able, go get other transportation
**MESMAC** Men who have sex with men
**MIGS** Men in grey suits (usually hospital administrators; see also WIGS)
**PAFO** P\*\*\*ed and fell over
**PIA** Partnership In Action / Personal-injury accident / Pain in the arse
**PITA** Pain in the arse
**POQ** P\*\*\* off quick (i.e. get out of a dangerous situation)

**RSN** Real soon now (i.e. the date when computer applications will be delivered)
**TEETH** Tried everything else, try homeopathy
**TLA** Three-letter acronym (like this one; looks good when written down, though)
**TLC** Tender loving care
**TMB** Too many birthdays
**TRO** Time ran out
**TTFO** Told to f**k off
**TTPO** Told to p*** off
**TUBE** Totally unnecessary breast examination
**WIGS** Women in grey suits

---

## FLAVOURS OF POTATO CRISPS

1. Cheese and Branston Pickle
2. Prawn Cocktail
3. Smokey Bacon
4. Sausage and Tomato
5. Salt and Vinegar
6. Baked Bean
7. Beef
8. Cheese and Onion
9. Bovril
10. Fizzy Fruit
11. Ready Salted
12. Minted Lamb
13. Beef and Onion
14. Marmite
15. Salt 'n' Shake
16. Four Cheese and Red Onion
17. Thai Sweet Chilli
18. Salt and Pepper
19. Barbecue
20. Salt and Malt Vinegar
21. Salt and Lineker
22. Cheese and Owen
23. Roast Chicken
24. Turkey and Paxo Stuffing
25. Worcester Sauce
26. Cheddar
27. Pickled Onion
28. Hedgehog
29. Jalfrezi
30. Big Breakfast
31. Steak
32. Cream Cheese and Spring Onion
33. Tomato
34. Fish and Chips
35. Ham and Mustard
36. Pizza

## SOME PRACTICAL HINTS

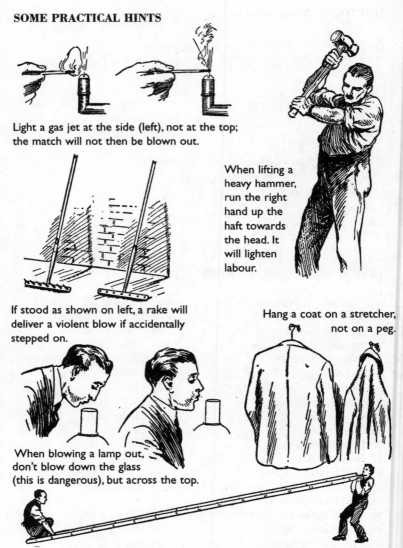

Light a gas jet at the side (left), not at the top; the match will not then be blown out.

When lifting a heavy hammer, run the right hand up the haft towards the head. It will lighten labour.

If stood as shown on left, a rake will deliver a violent blow if accidentally stepped on.

Hang a coat on a stretcher, not on a peg.

When blowing a lamp out, don't blow down the glass (this is dangerous), but across the top.

A ladder lifted in this way cannot slip, and will come up more easily.

## *DOCTOR WHO* ASSISTANTS

1. Susan Foreman (Carole Ann Ford)
2. Barbara Wright (Jacqueline Hill)
3. Ian Chesterton (William Russell)
4. Vicki (Maureen O'Brien)
5. Steven Taylor (Peter Purves)
6. Katarina (Adrienne Hill)
7. Sara Kingdom (Jean Marsh)
8. Dodo Chaplet (Jackie Lane)
9. Ben Jackson (Michael Craze)
10. Polly Wright (Anneke Wills)
11. Jamie (James Robert) McCrimmon (Frazer Hines)
12. Victoria Waterfield (Deborah Watling)
13. Zoë Herriott (Wendy Padbury)
14. Liz Shaw (Caroline John)
15. Jo Grant (Katy Manning)
16. Sarah Jane Smith (Elisabeth Sladen)
17. Harry Sullivan (Ian Marter)
18. Leela (Louise Jameson)
19. K9 (voice: John Leeson and David Brierley)
20. Romana (Romanadvoratrelundar) (Mary Tamm)
21. Romana  (after regeneration) (Lalla Ward)
22. Adric (Matthew Waterhouse)
23. Nyssa (Sarah Sutton)
24. Tegan Jovanka (Janet Fielding)
25. Turlough (Mark Strickson)
26. Kamelion (voice: Gerald Flood)
27. Peri (Perpugiliam) Brown (Nicola Bryant)
28. Erimem (Erimem ush Imteperem) (Caroline Morris)
29. Mel (Melanie) Bush (Bonnie Langford)
30. Frobisher (Robert Jezek)
31. Evelyn Smythe (Maggie Stables)
32. Ace (Sophie Aldred)
33. Benny (Bernice) Summerfield (Lisa Bowerman)
34. Antimony (Kevin Eldon)
35. Grace Holloway (Daphne Ashbrook)
36. Chang Lee (Yee Tse Tso)
37. Charley Pollard (India Fisher)
38. Ramsay (a vortisaur)
39. C'Rizz (pronounced 'Kerriz', like 'berries') (Conrad Westmaas)

## TEN PLACES NOT IN YORKSHIRE

Oxford
Cap Ferrat
Westward Ho!
Billericay
Ardnamurchan Point
Hayling Island
Birkenhead
Bandon (Co. Cork)
Callander
Rockall

## EXCEPTIONALLY SIMPLE PALINDROMES

nun
did
hah (exclamatory)
bib
mom (US)
pip
gag
tit (ornithol.)
Lil (proper name)
ere

## MOST POPULAR MISSING PERSONS

Osama bin-Laden
Captain L. E. G. 'Titus' Oates, Inniskilling Dragoons
Richard John Bingham, 7th Earl of Lucan
Martin Bormann
Stephen Fry
Amy Johnson
Josef Mengele
Commander 'Buster' Crabbe, RN
Agatha Christie
Saddam Hussein
Leslie Howard
Glenn Miller

## FOOD LOVERS

Anchovy and Cleopatra
Ham let and Oeuf elia
Lord Byron and Lady Caroline Lamb

Serrano and Roxanne
Troilus and Cress

## UNCOMMON EXPRESSIONS FOR EVERYDAY SOCIAL USE I

'No, she never got the hang of potty training.
Still hasn't, even at twelve'

'You could ask my husband. He won't know, though – he's really
rather stupid'

'In actual fact, I've put on seven pounds since Tuesday'

'You certainly don't earn much, do you?'

'Will I come to your party? No, of course not'

'You can send an e-mail if you want, but I shan't reply'

'Goodness, you are large, aren't you?'

'We know a marvellous little place. Well, I say "marvellous", but it's
actually rather horrible, and very dull'

'That new haircut of yours really is a disaster, isn't it?'

'Truth is, I'm just a rotten driver, like all men'

'Paris for the weekend? Good God, no – ghastly place'

---

## WORDS PREFIXED OR SUFFIXED 'ROYAL' THAT ARE NOT CONNECTED WITH THE BRITISH ROYAL FAMILY

royal jelly

*Royal Hunt of the Sun, The*

royal blue

royal fern

royal icing

royal mast

royal road to . . . , the

Kir royale

royal palm

royal antelope

royal (sail)

royal (stag)

royal purple

## MEMORABLE MOVIE LINES

I'm afraid of you. I've discovered you have an exciting mind,
something handsome men rarely have, and it might be too
much for me.
*Maggie Macnamara to Louis Jourdan in* Three Coins in a Fountain, *1954*

SULTAN SALADIN: May the seven doves rest on your shoulders.
SIR KENNETH: Doves? Or vultures? You slippery infidel!
*Rex Harrison and Laurence Harvey in* King Richard and the Crusaders, *1954*

If there is a god, I'd like to meet the dude, I'd like to go hang
out with him.
*Mickey Rourke in* Harley Davidson and the Marlboro Man, *1991*

Don't shout, I'm not deaf
*Albert Basserman as Ludwig van Beethoven in* The Melody Master, *1941*

You goddamned chauvinist pig ape!…You want to eat me?
Then go ahead.
*Jessica Lange in* King Kong, *1976*

Once they were men. Now they are land crabs.
Attack of the Crab Monsters, *1957*

Well, I've had enough of the unknown for one afternoon.
*Mara Corday in* Tarantula, *1955*

War! War! That's all you think of, Dick Plantagenet! You burner!
You pillager!
*Virginia Mayo to George Sanders in* King Richard and the Crusaders, *1954*

Oh, he'll be all right. He's got a bad blow on the head, suffering from
shock, mashed hands. But I can't find much other damage.
The Monster of Piedras Blancas, *1958*

When I'm sitting here with you, I don't even think about slime people…
*Hero to heroine in* The Slime People, *1962*

## THINGS NOT TO SAY TO YOUR MOTHER ON HER BIRTHDAY

Not dead then?

Gee, you must have been really old when you had me.

Is it a special day or something?

All of my friend's mothers look younger than you.

I would have baked you a cake but I had to dispose of a body.

Here are the keys to the home.

Have you thought of cosmetic surgery?

---

## 'THEIR NAME LIVETH FOR EVERMORE' I

**Colonel Tyler Rant** *(1816–76)* a cruel and ruthless Texas cattle baron, Colonel 'Ty' Rant gave his name not only to the noun 'tyrant', but to the verb 'to rant'

**Gustave Cliché** *(1694–1713)* French diarist, much given to repeating tired phrases in his interminable diaries of Court life. He died after eating a bad oyster, his doctors quite unable to understand his complaint that he had been poisoned by a 'succulent bivalve'

**Ernest 'Jelly' Jujube** *(1897–1953)* English confectioner, he invented the small sweet made from gelatin and sugar that still bears the nickname 'jujube'

**Amalia di Celli** *(c.1650–98)* astonishingly short-sighted Italian instrument maker, apprenticed to Antonio Stradivari; the apprentice-master's request that she make a violin as a test piece resulted, through her myopia, in an instrument eight times the size, and which bears her family name to this day

**Heinz-Jürgen Spritzer** *(1871–1936)* German inventor of the wine bar, he died from soda-water poisoning, probably caused by an infected drinking straw. In his memory, his favourite tipple – white wine mixed with soda water – was named after him

## CONTEMPORARY COLLECTIVE NOUNS

A smarm of sycophants

A leaning of left-wingers

An idleness of sloths

A brightness of spirits

A discontent of strikers

An absolution of priests

A press of journalists

A consideration of judges

A patience of saints

A crash of computers

An irritation of mobile phones

An undulation of limbo
   dancers

An anorexia of supermodels

A smirk of estate agents

A query of editors

An attitude of teenagers

A querulousness of pensioners

A decline of men

An ascension of women

An idiocy of reality TV contestants

A rant of road-ragers

A clinch of lovers

A swish of nuns

A loneliness of long-distance
   runners

---

## SAFETY GLOVES

chainmail gauntlets
extra grip and abrasion
  resistance
criss-cross coated
textured fingertips
flocked fishscale
reversed lozenge
natural rubber

## NICKNAMES FOR POLITICIANS

1. Iron Lady (Margaret Thatcher)
2. Hezza (Michael Heseltine)
3. Prezza (John Prescott)
4. Mandy (Peter Mandelson)
5. Rab Butler (R. A. Butler)
6. Tarzan (Michael Heseltine)
7. Dubya (George W. Bush)
8. Two Jags (John Prescott)

## 'THEIR NAME LIVETH FOR EVERMORE' II

**Richard Shonary** *(1711–53)* Irish wordsmith and wit, he was at work upon an English lexicon in advance of his great contemporary, Samuel Johnson, but died two years before the latter's *Dictionary* appeared, leaving his own uncompleted. Johnson immortalized Dick Shonary's name in the title he took for his own lexicon

**Miklós Kubist** *(1892–1970)* wealthy Hungarian amateur painter and art critic, his antipathy towards Braque and Picasso in the decade before the Great War led, in 1907, to them naming their budding artistic movement after him, purely as a tease

**The Marquess of Bap** *(1625–72)* Scottish soldier, sportsman and bon vivant who, nearly a century before the 4th Earl of Sandwich, asked his cook to serve his meat in a large, soft bread roll, as a snack that he could eat while salmon fishing. Unfairly, the resulting bread roll was named after Lord Bap, rather than the cook who devised it (and whose name has long since been lost to history)

**Frère (Xavier) Plosion** *(c.1210–c.1241)* Belgian monk and 'philosopher' (i.e. scientist), for a time employed as an assistant to the English philosopher and scientist Roger Bacon. In observing Bacon's experiments with gunpowder, Brother Xavier would sign his notes 'X. Plosion', thereby giving a noun to the language. His early death resulted from an imperfect understanding of the nature of volatile chemicals

**Stella Kroptopp** *(1974– )* Swiss-born fashion designer and head of design for the Fassace couture house. Fabulously mean, her desire to save on material led to the fashion for very short tops for women that leave the midriff bare, and which are named after her

---

## STRANGE PLACE NAMES IN THE USA AND CANADA

| | |
|---|---|
| Why, Arizona | Only, Tennessee |
| Difficult, Tennessee | Dildo, Newfoundland |
| Pardon, Maine | Blow Me Down, Newfoundland |

## ELVIS SIGHTINGS

### ELVIS IS A STRIPPER
*at Le Butt, a new strip club in Stroudsburg, Pennsylvania*
After several average men had strutted their respective stuff for us
Elvis appeared in a tight thong wearing a smile and blue suede shoes.
The crowd went nuts as Elvis gyrated and shook, as only the King
could. He was obviously an older man, but in the low lighting and
heavy make-up, he was a dream boat.

### ELVIS IS A MORTICIAN
*At Dunleavy's Funeral Home, Tampa, Florida*
We were greeted by a slight and obese older man, wearing a dark suit
and sunglasses trimmed in solid gold. He also had full silver-black
sideburns, and a thinning head of grey hair. We both slowly looked
behind us, shocked and surprised to see Elvis the mortician doing
that crazy dance with his arms out front and his knees bowed,
shaking left to right, again and again.

### ELVIS SELLS WATERBEDS
*at Sivle Yelserp, King Of Waterbeds, a supplier at the Millennium Mall in
Pittsburgh, Pennsylvania*
The bed was not on my mind as I took in the sight of this man who
was a dead ringer for Elvis Presley. Although a little chunky and
wrinkly, he had those sideburns, lips, and the blue suede shoes.

### ELVIS IS A DUCK!
It was different from the other ducks. It had on pants and a leather
jacket and blue suede shoes. I watched it dance and sing for a couple
of hours in front of a captivated duck audience. Then, Elvis the duck
got in his pink Cadillac and drove away.

### ELVIS SEEN AT 7/11
The other morning I stopped at the 7/ll in Miramar, Florida to get
some morning coffee...

### ELVIS SEEN AT LOCAL VIDEO STORE
He was looking through some old videos. Maybe he was looking for
some of his old films, to remember the good ol' times.

## FAMOUS MISCELLANEOUS BELGIANS

Hercule Poirot, fictional Belgian detective
Liz Claiborne, fashion designer
Johann Tserclaes Tilly, field marshal
Louis Hennepin, first European to explore the upper Mississippi river
Georges Rémi, better known as Hergé, the creator of 'Tin-Tin' (Kuifje)
Pierre Culliford, alias 'Peyo', the creator of 'The Smurfs'
Andre Franquin, creator of the 'Guust Flater' and 'Marsupilami' comic series
Henri-Marie Lafontaine, winner of the 1913 Nobel Peace Prize
Christophe Plantin, bookbinder, printer and typographer
Dominique Pire, winner of the 1958 Nobel Peace Prize
Dries van Noten, fashion designer
Ann Demeulemeester, fashion designer
Dirk Frimout, the first Belgian astronaut
Walter Arfeuille, Guinness record holder – lifted 281.5kg a distance of 17cm
   off the ground with his teeth in 1990

---

## RADICAL BUILDING MATERIALS

| | | | |
|---|---|---|---|
| brushed nylon | wattle and daub | butter | cellophane |
| gravel | mashed potato | gelatin | ivory |
| cow dung | winceyette | | |

---

## 'DO YOU COME HERE OFTEN?' AND OTHER OPENING GAMBITS

Do you have a map? I keep getting lost in your eyes.

If I could rewrite the alphabet, I would put U and I together.

You are the star that completes the constellation of my existence.

Is your daddy a thief? So who stole the stars out of the sky and put
them in your eyes?

Do you believe in love at first sight, or should I walk by again?

## MAFIA NICKNAMES

| Name | Nickname | Family |
|------|----------|--------|
| Anthony Spilotro | 'Tony the Ant' | Chicago |
| Joseph Pignatelli | 'Joe Pig' | |
| Salvatore Gravano | 'Sammy the Bull' | Gambino |
| Paul Ricca | 'The Waiter' | Chicago |
| Sam DeStefano | 'Mad Sam' | Chicago |
| Frank Rosenthal | 'Lefty' | Las Vegas |
| Frank Abbandando | 'The Dasher' | |
| Jimmy Burke | 'The Gent' | Chicago |
| Albert Anastasia | 'The Mad Hatter' | |
| Otto Berman | 'Abbadabba' | |
| Tommy Brown | 'Three Fingers' | |
| Louis Delenhauser | 'Cop Out' | |
| Vito Gurino | 'Socko' | |
| Angelo McConnach | 'Sonny Bamboo' | |
| Frankie Manzo | 'The Wop' | |
| Joe Manri | 'Buddha' | |
| Ben Siegel | 'Bugsy' | Costello |
| Vito Vario | 'Tuddy' | New York |
| Jacob Shapiro | 'Gurrah' | |
| Jimmy Torello | 'The Turk' | Chicago |
| Alphonse Tarricone | 'Funzi' | |
| Jackie D'Amico | 'Nose' | Chicago |
| Jack Giordano | 'Handsome Jack' | Chicago |
| Amato Baldassare | 'Baldo' | |
| Stefano Cannone | 'Stevie Beef' | |
| James Capesso | 'Fort Lee Jimmy' | |
| Phillip Alderisio | 'Milwaukee Phil' | |
| Joseph Aiuppa | 'Joey Doves' | |
| Donald Angelini | 'The Wizard of Odds' | |
| William Daddano | 'Potatoes' | |
| Ronnie DeAngelis | 'Balloon Head' | |
| Carl DeLuna | 'Toughy' | |
| Michael DeFeo | 'Iron Mike' | |
| Sam Giancana | 'Mooney' | |
| John Cerasani | 'Boobie' | |
| Sally D'Ottavio | 'Paintglass' | |

| James Episcopia | 'Jimmy Legs' | |
| Salvatore Farrugia | 'Sally Fruits' | |
| Dominick Napolitano | 'Sonny Black' | |
| Charles Panarella | 'Charlie Moose' | |
| Alphonse Persico | 'Allie Boy' | |
| Anthony Rabito | 'Mr Fish' | |
| Anthony Salerno | 'Fat Tony' | |
| Antonio Tamasulo | 'Boots' | |
| Dominick Trinchera | 'Big Trin' | |
| Willie Alderman | 'Ice Pick' | |
| Anthony Joseph Accardo | 'Joe Batters, Big Tuna' | Chicago |
| Johnny Masiello | 'Gentleman' | |
| John Gotti | 'The Dapper Don', 'The Teflon Don', 'Mr Untouchable' | Gambino |
| Giuseppe Masseria | 'Joe the Boss' | |
| Tony Rampino | 'Roach' | |
| Richie Boiardo | 'The Boot' | |
| Frank Carrone | 'Buzzy' | |
| Martin Cassella | 'Motts' | |
| Anthony Casso | 'Gas Pipe' | |
| Phillip Cestaro | 'Philly Broadway' | |
| Vincent Gigante | 'The Chin' | Genovese |
| Michael Coppola | 'Trigger Mike' | |
| Anthony Corallo | 'Tony Ducks' | |
| Michael Falciano | 'The Falcon' | |
| Carmine Fatico | 'Charlie Wags' | |
| Ralphie Galione | 'Wigs' | |
| Joseph Gioelli | 'Joe Jelly' | |
| Frank Guidice | 'Frankie the Beard' | |

---

## NEW ZEALAND INVENTIONS

The self-sealing lid
The wide-toothed shearing comb
Velcro
The luggage carousel
Pavlova

The stamp-vending machine
The bobby pin
The electric fence
The jet boat

## SAFETY FIRST (SEE LEFT)

1. How not to carry a gun.
2. Don't chop wood on a hollow surface.
3. Be careful when stepping off the kerb in crowded streets.
4. Don't step out from behind a vehicle without reconnoitring.
5. Beware of belts and of parts of machinery in motion.
6. Don't try to slip between vehicles travelling in opposite directions.
7. Don't press in the ball of a mineral-water bottle with your thumb.
8. Cover up a bottle of effervescing liquid before drawing the cork.
9. Beware of grass slopes in dry weather.
10. Don't dive into water of unknown depth.
11. Keep your feet together when lifting heavy weights.

---

## POPULAR BUMBLEBEES RESIDENT IN THE BRITISH ISLES

*Bombus pomodorus*          *Bombus humilis*
*Bombus tilensis*           *Bombus hortorum*
*Bombus pascuorum*          *Bombus pratorum*
*Bombus terrestris*         *Bombus lapidaries*
*Bombus ruderarius*
*Bombus lucorum* (and *Bombus magnus,* of course)

---

## MUCH LESS POPULAR BUMBLEBEES RESIDENT IN THE BRITISH ISLES

*Bombus monticola*          *Bombus jonellus*
*Bombus soroeensis*         *Bombus muscorum*
*Bombus ruderatus*          *Bombus sylvarum*
*Bombus arctorum* (for a social insect, old *B. arctorum* is pretty anti-social)
*Bombus subterraneus* (well, what does it expect? – it hasn't been seen in
    this country since 1988)

## A SELECTION OF ADVERTISING SLOGANS

Ah! **Bisto**

Beanz meanz **Heinz**

Snap Crackle and Pop (Kelloggs **Rice Krispies**)

They're GREEEAT! (Kelloggs **Frosties**)

For Mash get **Smash** (Cadburys)

Are you a **Cadbury's Fruit and Nut** case?

All because the lady loves **Milk Tray** (Cadburys)

Graded Grains Make Finer Flour (**Homepride**)

Don't forget the fruit gums mum! (**Rowntree**)

A **Double Diamond** works wonders

**Heineken** reaches the parts that other beers cannot reach

Bet he drinks **Carling Black Label**

What we want is **Watneys**

You're never alone with a **Strand** (cigarettes)

Cool as a mountain stream (**Consulate** cigarettes)

You'll be a little lovelier each day, with fabulous pink **Camay**

**1001** cleans a big, big carpet for less than half-a-crown

You'll wonder where the yellow went when you brush your teeth
with **Pepsodent**

## UNCOMMON EXPRESSIONS FOR EVERYDAY SOCIAL USE II

'Actually, we find he's not at all bright for his age'

'To be honest, I think you look a fright in all of them'

'No thanks – I loathe gardens'

'Like most Irishmen, he's extremely unfunny and wholly charmless'

'It's patently obvious that the weapons of mass destruction
are in Iraq'

'I don't actually care that you mind if I smoke; I'm still going to'

'Turn round. Yes, as I thought: if anything, it looks even
bigger in that outfit'

'No, I'm not at all busy that night. I just don't want to come'

'What a horrid car! Foul colour, too. Is it yours?'

'Let's face it, Camilla's the best thing that ever happened
to the royal family'

---

## TEN THINGS TO TAKE ON HOLIDAY

a cucumber
the Encyclopaedia Britannica
the man next door
a llama
measles
a ball of garden twine
jelly
a cold haddock
a week's worth of old newspapers
one trainer (without laces)

## BRITISH BOLLARDS – SOME COMMON TYPES

socketed
chain-linked
surface-fixing
reinforced
impact-resistant
impact-absorbing
self-returning
cycle-parking
lockable (parking post)
cannon-style

## AN ALPHABETICAL POEM

### The Siege of Belgrade

An Austrian army, awfully arrayed,
Boldly by battery besieged Belgrade.
Cossack commanders cannonading come,
Dealing destruction's devastating doom.
Every endeavour engineers essay,
For fame, for fortune fighting – furious fray!
Generals 'gainst generals grapple – gracious God!
How honours Heaven heroic hardihood!
Infuriate, indiscriminate in ill,
Kindred kill kinsmen, kinsmen kindred kill.
Labour low levels longest, loftiest lines;
Men march 'mid mounds, 'mid moles, 'mid murderous mines;
Now noxious, noisy numbers nothing, naught
Of outward obstacles, opposing ought;
Poor patriots, partly purchased, partly pressed,
Quite quaking, quickly 'Quarter! Quarter!' quest.
Reason returns, religious right redounds,
Suwarrow stops such sanguinary sounds.
Truce to thee, Turkey! Triumph to thy train,
Unwise, unjust, unmerciful Ukraine!
Vanish vain victory! vanish, victory vain!
Why wish we warfare? Wherefore welcome were
Xerxes, Ximenes, Xanthus, Xavier?
Yield, yield, ye youths! Ye yeomen, yield your yell!
Zeus', Zarpater's, Zoroaster's zeal,
Attracting all, arms against acts appeal!
ALARIC ALEXANDER WATTS (1799-1864)

---

## VERY UNPOPULAR BUMBLEBEES RESIDENT IN THE UK

| | | |
|---|---|---|
| *Bombus terribilis* | *Bombus paedophilius* | *Bombus horribilis* |
| *Bombus ineptus* | *Bombus noxius* | *Bombus depravatus* |
| *Bombus inebrius* | *Bombus insanus* | *Bombus mendax* |
| *Bombus fraudulentus* | | |

## DECLINING ENGLISH SURNAMES

Weakitharm
Fondlebum
Spit
Saxe-Coburg und Gotha
Wibble
Cnut

Butterscotch-Orgasm
  (pron. 'Booterham')
Titpolly
Shagnasty
Polabare

---

## THE SEMAPHORE ALPHABET

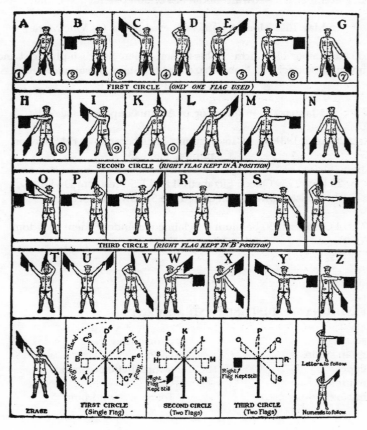

## EXCEPTIONALLY DULL DATES

29 July 1959 Postcodes introduced in Britain

29 February 1904 A White Paper was published stating that the British colonies preferred a decimal system to the Imperial one

1 September 1830 In Boston, Mass., Sarah J. Hales published her poem 'Mary Had a Little Lamb'

12 December 1769 Edward Beran of London patented Venetian blinds

6 May 1642 Montreal officially established (as Ville Marie)

30 November 1869 Birth of Nils Gustaf Dalen, Swedish physicist and inventor, winner of a Nobel Prize for his automatic sun valve used on buoys and lighthouses

11 January 1946 King Zog of Albania deposed *in absentia*

20 April 1981 Steve 'Interesting' Davis became World Snooker Champion, aged 23

26 June 1959 Queen Elizabeth II and US President Dwight D. Eisenhower inaugurated the St Lawrence Seaway

14 October 1830 Belgium proclaimed an independent kingdom

---

## FASHIONABLE DISEASES AND AILMENTS

| | |
|---|---|
| scrapie | pyorrhoea |
| groin strain | DOA |
| gapes | sympathetic pregnancy |
| mildew | UDN |
| myxomatosis | Tourette's syndrome |

## THE TOP EIGHTEEN MOST ELIGIBLE, FUNNY, FASCINATING AND INCREDIBLY CHARMING PEOPLE (PROBABLY)

Paul Henderson
Mike Brookes-Sullivan
Andy Roberts
Joan the Baptiste
Jenny Heller
Techno Ted Funnel
Sharon Gurney
Kim Bishop
Al Capone
Bob Gilbey

David Pearson
John of Arc
Scott Chowen
Kingsley Dawson
Peter Mandelson
Louise Hunter
Jan Watson
David Llewellyn
Patrick Jeffrey
Mother Teresa of Calcutta

---

## FLOPPED BOOK AND FILM SEQUELS

*Spatula: Son of the Vampire*

*The Broken Rope: The Return of Tess of the D'Urbervilles*

*Smaller Band of Brothers*

*Private Ryan Finally Cops It*

*The Postgraduate*

*Jungle Book III: The Death of Baloo*

*A Streetcar Named Cemetery*

*Midnight's Children's Children*

*The Sun Also Sets (After It's Risen)*

*The Death of Pi: The Tiger's Revenge*

## USEFUL 'FRANGLAIS' PHRASES
## (AS SPOKEN IN NORTHERN ONTARIO)

la waitress a porte sés jeans bin tight

sick-malade, no can travaille

on é trop back-loggé

as-tu booké ton time-off pour Noël?

y'a dés belles buns

c'weekend, j'suis off

y'm'a stressé right-out

trois takeout, s.v.p

j'ai lés munchies

j'aime pas l'mascara sur tés yeux

le stripper a enlevé sa G-string!

mon coat é half-price, més jeans é two-for-one

Florida, c'é une trip assez-cheap

c'é pas corrêct, j'va l'scratché-out

j'ai dés gants d'rubber

tu vas être groundé

mon bloodpressure est skyhigh!

c'é lights-out pour moi

## HEAD DIVISIONS

A. Main intellect      B. Sympathies/loyalty/devotion
C. Safeguarding        D. Functioning of the mind
E. Instincts            F. Sexual      G. Social

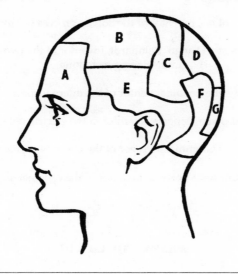

## WEBSITES OFFERING NEW ZEALAND TRIVIA

www.geocities.com/TheTropics/1779/trivia.htm
www.goway.com/downunder/newzealand/nz_trivia.html
www.funtrivia.com/dir/4376.html
www.idec2003.com/new_zealand_trivia.htm
www.immigrationvisa.org/new_zealand_trivia.htm
www.websterschools.org/classrooms/ state_library/australia.html
www.ciri.hypermart.net/new_zealand_trivia.htm
www.cchsigs.org/igs/zealand.htm
www.zesprikiwi.com/pressarchive.htm
www.huntindia.com/immigration/new-zealand/why-NZ/nz-
   trivia.asp

## FAMOUS BELGIAN INVENTORS

Gerardus Mercator, cartographer, mathematician and geographer

Joseph Plateau, inventor of the stroboscope

Ernest Solvay, inventor of the Solvay process (ammonia)

Jean Baptiste 'Django' Reinhardt, inventor of the two-finger
guitar-playing technique

Jean Joseph Étienne Lenoir, inventor of the internal-combustion engine

Charles van Depoele, inventor of the electric railway

Zénobe Gramme, inventor of the Gramme dynamo

Constant Loiseau, inventor of the optometer

---

## MAXIMS FOR LIFE III

When cycling in hilly country, inspect the brakework frequently.

A good lathering means a clean shave.

When travelling, distribute your money about your person.

Successful litigation is often less ruinous than failure.

Don't write an angry letter even if you have good cause for anger.

Lose an hour in the morning and you will be hunting for it all day.

Don't wash a dog oftener than is absolutely necessary.

Take advantage of hot summer weather to do any tarring required.

## BUOYS USED BY VARIOUS NATIONS

### UNITED KINGDOM

*(a) (b)* *Port Hand, or Left hand entering River or Estuary from Seaward. Can buoys (a) or (b)*

*(a) (b) Middle Grounds (a) outer end (b) inner end White horizontal Stripes. Spherical buoys*

*Starboard Hand or Right hand entering River or Estuary from Seaward- Conical buoys*

### FRANCE

*Port Hand col=Black, with Can on Staff. Uneven Numbers from seaward*

*Middle Grounds White and Black Horizontal Stripes & 2 Cones*

*Starboard Hand-Red with cone on staff. Even Nos from Seaward*

### GERMANY

*(a) (b) Port Hand Black Conical Buoys as (a) or (b)*

*(a) (b) Middle Grounds as at (a) or (b) Spherical with Horizontal Stripes*

*(a) (b) Starboard Hand (a) Red Spar- or (b) Can Buoys*

PORT HAND

STARBOARD HAND

INNER END

MIDDLE GROUND

OUTER END

BELL 'SPECIAL BUOY (POSITION)

*Sketch showing how a British Estuary is buoyed*

### RUSSIA

*White Spar and Black Broom-North of Danger*

*Red Spar & Red Broom South of Danger*

*Red & White Spar & Two Brooms East*

*Black & White Spar & Two Brooms West*

### HOLLAND & BELGIUM

*Port Hand Black Can Buoys*

*Middle Grounds One Colour or Red & Black Stripes*

*Starboard Hand Red Conical Buoys*

*Gas Buoy*

OVH

*Bell Buoy*

*To mark the position of a wreck (painted Green)*

*Whistling Buoy*

*Some Types of British Buoys used to mark Special Positions*

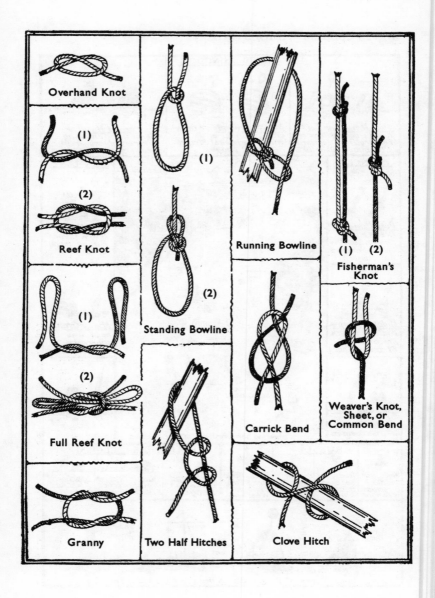

Overhand Knot

(1)

(2)

Reef Knot

(1)

(2)

Full Reef Knot

Granny

(1)

(2)

Standing Bowline

Two Half Hitches

Running Bowline

Carrick Bend

Clove Hitch

(1) (2)

Fisherman's Knot

Weaver's Knot, Sheet, or Common Bend

## SOME USEFUL KNOTS, HITCHES, ETC.
## FOR COMMUTERS (SEE LEFT)

[The end of a rope is indicated by a dark 'serving' of twine; the ragged end indicates where the main, or 'standing,' part of the rope is broken away for illustrative purposes.] The Reef Knot, Full Reef Knot, the Carrick Bend, the Fisherman's Knot and the Sheet Bend are used for fastening two ropes, etc., together. The Fisherman's Knot is a favourite with anglers for tying gut. In making the Sheet Bend, loop the end of one rope, and pass the end of the other through and round the loop, and between the loop and its own "standing" part. The Standing Bowline (much used by sailors) gives a loop which will not slip under strain. The Running Bowline is a good self-tightener. The Two Half Hitches and the Clove Hitch are simple methods of attaching a rope to an object without the use of a knot. The two turns of the Clove Hitch are brought close together after being formed as shown in the illustration.

## SOME OTHER USEFUL KNOTS AND HITCHES

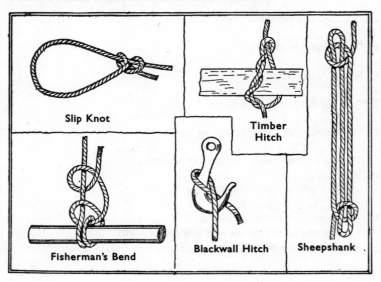

Slip Knot

Timber Hitch

Fisherman's Bend

Blackwall Hitch

Sheepshank

**THE LAWYER'S AN ASS**

'Now, doctor, isn't it true that when a person dies in his sleep, he doesn't know anything about it until the next morning?'

'The youngest son, the twenty-year-old, how old is he?'

'Were you present when your picture was taken?'

'Were you alone or by yourself?'

'Was it you or your younger brother who was killed in the war?'

'Did he kill you?'

'How far apart were the vehicles at the time of the collision?'

'You were there until the time that you left, is that true?'

'Doctor, how many autopsies have you performed on dead people?'

Q: 'She had three children, right?'
A: 'Yes.'
Q: 'How many were boys?'
A: 'None.'
Q: 'Were there any girls?'

Q: 'You say the stairs went down to the basement?'
A: 'Yes.'
Q: 'And these stairs, did they go up also?'

Q: 'How was your first marriage terminated?'
A: 'By death.'
Q: 'And by whose death was it terminated?'

Q: 'Can you describe the individual?'
A: 'He was about medium height and had a beard.'
Q: 'Was this a male or a female?'

Q: 'Do you recall the time that you examined the body?'
A: 'The autopsy started around 8.30pm.'
Q: 'And Mr Hubert was dead at the time?'

Q: 'Mr Slattery, you went on a rather elaborate honeymoon, didn't you?'
A: 'I went to Europe, sir.'
Q: 'And you took your new wife?'

Q: 'So the date of conception was August eighth?'
A: 'Yes.'
Q: 'And what were you doing at the time?'

Q: 'Are you qualified to give a urine sample?'
A: 'I have been since early childhood.'

Q: 'Doctor, before you performed the autopsy, did you check for a pulse?'
A: 'No.'
Q: 'Did you check for blood pressure?'
A: 'No.'
Q: 'Did you check for breathing?'
A: 'No.'
Q: 'So, then it is possible that the patient was alive when you began the autopsy?'
A: 'No.'
Q: 'How can you be so sure, Doctor?'
A: 'Because his brain was sitting on my desk in a jar.'
Q: 'But could the patient have still been alive nevertheless?'
A: 'It's possible he could have been alive, and practising law somewhere, I suppose.'

---

## NOTORIOUS CEREAL KILLERS

Lennie Kellogg
'Captain' Oats
Gräfin Erika von Muesli
Hiram B. Grapenut
Sam and Fiona Frosty

Ernest Porridge
Fenella Poptart
Jim 'Golden' Graham
Henry Crunch
Deirdre Shreddie

## THINGS THEY MAY WISH THEY HAD NEVER SAID

'Read my lips, no new taxes.'
*George Bush, senior, 1988, eighteen months before he raised taxes and four years before he lost the 1992 election to Bill Clinton*

'Believe me, Germany is unable to wage war.'
*David Lloyd George, former British prime minister, 1934*

'I have no more territorial ambition in Europe.'
*Adolf Hitler, 1939, three months before invading Poland*

'No woman will in my time be prime minister.'
*Margaret Thatcher, British politician and future prime minister, 1969*

'I have no political ambition for myself or for my children.'
*Joseph P. Kennedy, 1936 (father of John F., Bobby and Teddy Kennedy)*

'I promise that truth shall be the policy of the Nixon administration.'
*Spiro Agnew, Vice-President, 1968*

'We keep a vigil of peace around the world.'
*Lyndon B. Johnson, US Vice-President, May 1968, as the US was sending 'military advisers' to South Vietnam*

'You will be home before the leaves have fallen from the trees.'
*Wilhelm II, German Kaiser, August 1914, to his troops at the beginning of World War I, which went on for over four years*

'The culmination and final war for human liberty.'
*Woodrow Wilson, US president, January 1918, predicting that World War I would be the last global war*

'I want to say one thing to the American people. I want you to listen to me. I'm going to say this again: I did not have sexual relations with that woman, Miss Lewinsky.'
*Bill Clinton, US President, January 1998*

## POPULAR ASSAULT RIFLES

| | |
|---|---|
| M16 | 5.56-mm calibre; USA |
| FAMAS | 5.56-mm calibre; France |
| SA80/84 | 5.56-mm calibre; Great Britain |
| AK-47 | 7.62-mm calibre; Soviet Union |
| M1 Garand | .30-inch calibre; USA |
| M4 carbine | 5.56-mm calibre; USA/Israel |
| G36K | 5.56-mm calibre; Germany |
| SLR (L1A1) | 7.62-mm calibre; Belgium/Great Britain |
| AK-74 | 5.56-mm calibre; Soviet Union |
| G3 | 7.62-mm calibre; Germany |

---

## WORDS DERIVING FROM ALLEGED NATIONAL OR REGIONAL CHARACTERISTICS

**welsh** — (also welch) to fail to honour an agreement, debt or obligation (from Wales, Welsh)

**scotch** — to halt, impede, thwart, deny etc. ('scotch' is an English contraction of 'Scottish')

**b\*\*\*er** — from Bulgar, Bulgarian, originally meaning a heretic (Bulgarians were often held to be heretics, since they followed the Orthodox, rather than Roman Catholic, Church; heresy was associated with forbidden sexual practices, such as sodomy)

**swede** — root vegetable; first imported into Britain from Sweden

**French letter** — condom (Condom is a town in SW France, although the connection has never been proved)

**Dutch cap** — contraceptive diaphragm (possibly from a supposed resemblance to the headgear)

**Spanish practice** — irregular, if not illegal, working practice (from alleged habits of Spanish workers)

**Dutch treat** — occasion at which each pays for himself (from the supposed parsimony of Dutch people)

**gothic** — originally, 'not classical' (from the Goths, a Germanic people that invaded the Roman empire between the third and fifth centuries)

## MOVIE TITLES INVOLVING ANIMALS/BIRDS

*One Flew Over the Cuckoo's Nest*
*Cat People*
*Straw Dogs*
*The Pink Panther*
*The Eagle Has Landed*
*Poor Cow*
*The Mouse That Roared*
*The Hound of the Baskervilles*
*The Day of the Jackal*
*To Kill a Mockingbird*
*The Lion in Winter*
*Dog Day Afternoon*
*A Man Called Horse*
*What's New Pussycat*
*Dances With Wolves*
*Black Hawk Down*
*Anaconda*
*King Rat*
*Silence of the Lambs*
*Raging Bull*
*K9*
*Crocodile Dundee*
*The Dogs of War*
*Cat on a Hot Tin Roof*

---

## CAT WORDS

| | |
|---|---|
| catalogue | catastrophe |
| cataract | catamaran |
| catapult | catatonia |
| catechism | catarrh |
| category | catcall |
| catafalque | catalyst |
| cataclysm | catacomb |

## THE SEVEN AGES OF MAN
## (ACCORDING TO SHAKESPEARE)

The infant, mewling and puking in his nurse's arms
The whining schoolboy, creeping like snail unwillingly to school
The lover, sighing like furnace, with a woeful ballad made to his
  mistress' eyebrow
The soldier, full of strange oaths, seeking the bubble reputation even
  in the cannon's mouth
The justice, in fair round belly, full of wise saws and modern
  instances
The pantaloon, lean and slippered, with spectacles on nose, his big
  manly voice turning again towards childish treble
Second childishness and mere oblivion, sans teeth, sans eyes, sans
  taste, sans everything

*As You Like It*, II: 7

---

## OR, TO PUT IT ANOTHER WAY:

Seven ages, first puking and mewling,
Then very p***ed off with one's schooling,
Then f**ks, and then fights,
Then judging chaps' rights;
Then sitting in slippers; then drooling.

VICTOR GRAY, 'The Seven Ages of Man'

---

## MAGAZINES FOR SPECIALIST INTERESTS

| | | |
|---|---|---|
| *Angels on Earth* | *Magic Crochet* | *Funeral Director* |
| *Aquarian Times* | *Fangoria* | *The Ferret* |
| *Charisma* | *Veranda* | *Knives Illustrated* |
| *SpiritLed Woman* | *Fate* | *Toy Farmer* |
| *Discerner* | *Truckin'* | *Bulletin of the String* |
| *Earnest Christian* | *Birds and Blooms* | *Figure Association* |
| *Shaman* | *Nuts and Volts* | *Big Reel* |
| *Flame* | *Fur, Fish and Game* | *Spoon* |
| *Mental Floss* | *Reminisce* | |

## MOVIE TITLES INVOLVING CITIES

*The Philadelphia Story*
*Chicago*
*An American Werewolf in London*
*Last Tango in Paris*
*Sleepless in Seattle*
*Mission to Moscow*
*Our Man in Havana*
*Meet Me in St Louis*
*Tokyo Joe*
*The Las Vegas Story*
*New York, New York*
*Macau*
*Paris, Texas*
*Funeral in Berlin*
*Death in Venice*
*Crocodile Dundee*

---

## AIRCRAFT ENGINES NAMED AFTER BIRDS
## AND ANIMALS (SOME MYTHICAL)

Wolseley Viper
Rolls-Royce Eagle
Armstrong-Siddeley Puma
Rolls-Royce Griffon
Rolls-Royce Kestrel
Rolls-Royce Merlin
Rolls-Royce Vulture
Bristol Pegasus
Rolls-Royce Falcon
Rolls-Royce Hawk

---

## MAXIMS FOR LIFE IV

Appetite is a good sauce and variety is another.

Oil and dry heat are very injurious to india-rubber.

## SOME TITLES TAKEN FROM SHAKESPEARE

J. M. Barrie, *Dear Brutus* (play; *Julius Caesar*)

H. E. Bates, *The Darling Buds of May* (novel; Sonnet XVIII)

Alfred Duff Cooper, *Old Men Forget* (autobiography; *Henry V*)

Noël Coward, *Present Laughter* (play; *Twelfth Night*)

Noël Coward, *This Happy Breed* (play; *Richard II*)

William Faulkner, *The Sound and the Fury* (novel; *Macbeth*)

Aldous Huxley, *Brave New World* (novel; *The Tempest*)

Rose Macaulay, *Told By an Idiot* (novel; *Macbeth*)

Somerset Maugham, *Cakes and Ale* (novel; *Twelfth Night*)

Marcel Proust (tr. C. K. Scott Moncrieff), *Remembrance of Things Past* (novel; Sonnet XXX)

Terence Rattigan, *Who Is Silvia?* (play; *The Two Gentlemen of Verona*)

Julian Slade, *Salad Days* (musical; *Antony and Cleopatra*)

John Steinbeck, *The Moon is Down* (novel; *Macbeth*)

Frederick Forsyth, *The Dogs of War* (novel; *Julius Caesar*)

---

## THREE-LETTER ANIMALS

| | |
|---|---|
| gnu | hen |
| elk | pig |
| owl | cow |
| cat | rat |
| dog | eel |

## SOME USEFUL STATISTICS

In Britain, one out of every four potatoes is eaten in the form of chips

27 per cent of female lottery winners hide their winning tickets in their bras

Men are more likely to be colour blind than women

The city of Las Vegas has the most hotel rooms in the world

On average, a car driver will swear at least 32,000 times in their lifetime while driving

96 per cent of candles are purchased by women

Children laugh about 400 times a day, while adults laugh on average only 15 times a day

In a lifetime, the average driver will honk 15,250 times

It is estimated that at any one time, 0.7 per cent of the world's population is drunk

Roughly 44 per cent of junk mail is thrown away unopened

---

## SIXTEEN SHEEP BREEDS YOU MAY NOT HAVE HEARD OF

Barbados Blackbelly
Beulah Speckled-Face
Castlemilk Moorit
Exmoor Horn
Finnsheep
Gromark
Hog Island
Kajli

Kooka
Mouflon
Norwegian Fur
Polypay
Scotch Blackface
Tuj
West African Dwarf
Yoroo

## FAMOUS PEOPLE WITH PSEUDONYMS

*Jennifer Aniston* – Jennifer Anistonapoulos
*Adam Ant* – Stuart Leslie Goddard
*Michael Caine* – Maurice J. Micklewhite
*Lewis Carroll* – Charles Lutwidge Dodgson
*Chubby Checker* – Ernest Evans
*Eric Clapton* – Eric Patrick Clap
*Bette Davis* – Ruth Elizabeth Davis
*Snoop Doggy Dogg* – Calvin Broadus
*Diana Dors* – Diana Fluck
*Samantha Fox* – Stacia Micula
*Ava Gardner* – Lucy Johnson
*Judy Garland* – Frances Ethel Gumm
*Lillian Gish* – Lillian de Guiche
*Cary Grant* – Archibald Alexander Leach
*Alec Guinness* – Alec Guinness de Cuffe
*Rita Hayworth* – Margarita Carmen Cansino
*Harry Houdini* – Ehrich Weiss
*Elton John* – Reginald Kenneth Dwight
*Spike Jones* – Lindley Armstrong Jones
*Boris Karloff* – William Henry Pratt
*Michael Keaton* – Michael Douglas
*Ben Kingsley* – Krishna Banji
*Veronica Lake* – Constance Frances Marie Ockelman
*Bruce Lee* – Lee Jun Fan
*Peggy Lee* – Norma Engstrom
*Marilyn Manson* – Brian Warner
*Meat Loaf* – Marvin Lee Aday
*Billy Ocean* – Leslie Sebastian Charles
*Iggy Pop* – James Newell Osterberg
*Ginger Rogers* – Virginia Katherine McMath
*Roy Rogers* – Leonard Franklin Slye
*Peter Sellers* – Richard Henry Sellers
*Omar Sharif* – Michael Shalhoub Prizhivago
*Martin Sheen* – Ramón Estevez
*Gene Vincent* – Eugene Vincent Craddock
*Natalie Wood* – Natasha Nikolaevna Zacharenko-Gurdin

## HOW TO SATISFY A WOMAN

Adore, appreciate, beguile, captivate, caress, charm, cherish, coax,
commit to, compliment, console, delight, embrace, empathize, enchant,
enthral, hug, humour, idolize, indulge, massage, nuzzle, palpitate,
pamper, phone, placate, promise, relish, respect, sacrifice for, savour,
serenade, spoil, stroke, treasure, understand, venerate, worship

## HOW TO SATISFY A MAN

Show up naked

## WORKING MOVIE TITLES

*Annie Hall* – Anhedonia
*Bed of Roses* – Amelia and the King of Plants
*Casablanca* – Rick's Place
*Clueless* – I Was A Teenage Teenager
*ET* – A Boy's Life
*The Full Monty* – Eggs, Beans and Chippendales
*A Hard Day's Night* – Beatlemania
*Help!* – Eight Arms To Hold You
*It's a Wonderful Life* – The Greatest Gift
*North by Northwest* – The Man on Lincoln's Nose
*Some Like it Hot* – Not Tonight, Josephine
*Tootsie* – Would I Lie To You?
*While You Were Sleeping* – Coma Guy

## SOME WORDS BEGINNING WITH OVER

| | | |
|---|---|---|
| overview | overflow | overtone |
| overrated | overcome | overboard |
| oversexed | overtime | overload |
| overarm | overlook | overdue |

## NOT WILDLY POPULAR SEA CAPTAINS

Captain William Bligh, RN, HMS *Bounty*

Captain Edward J. Smith, White Star liner RMS *Titanic*

Captain Robert Falcon Scott, RN, National Antarctic Expedition vessels *Discovery*, then *Terra Nova*

Captain Queeg, USN, USS *Caine* (in Herman Wouk's Pulitzer Prize-winning novel *The Caine Mutiny*, 1951)

Captain Stanley Lord, SS *Californian* which, though in the vicinity, failed to go to the rescue of the stricken *Titanic*

Rt Hon. Sir Edward Heath, KG, MBE, yacht *Morning Cloud*

Kapitänleutnant Walther Schweiger, U-20, whose U-boat torpedoed the Cunard liner RMS *Lusitania* off the south coast of Ireland, 7 May 1915, with the loss of more than 1,000 lives, 124 of them citizens of the then neutral United States

Captain Ahab, whaler *Pequod* (in Herman Melville's novel *Moby-Dick*, 1851)

Captain Benjamin S. Briggs, half-brig *Mary Céleste* (originally *Amazon*), found drifting and abandoned, 5 December 1872

Captain George Pollard Jr, Nantucket whaler *Essex*, rammed and sunk by an enraged sperm whale in the Pacific, 20 November 1820. The tale inspired Melville's *Moby-Dick* (see above)

---

## TEN THREE-LETTER WORDS INVOLVING MOVEMENT

| | | | |
|---|---|---|---|
| bob | run | jog | bop |
| hop | jig | fly | row |
| jet | ski | | |

## TWELVE COMMON MISQUOTATIONS

**Pride goes before a fall** – Pride goeth before destruction, and an haughty spirit before a fall

**Fresh fields and pastures new** – Tomorrow to fresh woods and pastures new

**To gild the lily** – To gild refined gold, to paint the lily

**By the skin of my teeth** – I am escaped with the skin of my teeth

**Thin red line** – Thin red streak, tipped with a line of steel

**A poor thing, but my own** – An ill-favoured thing, sir, but mine own

**A plain unvarnished tale** – I will a round, unvarnished tale deliver

**Beam me up, Scotty** – Beam us up, Mr Scott

**Play it again, Sam** – Play it, Sam. Play 'As Time Goes By'. *Or*, If she can stand it, I can. Play it!

**Take away these baubles** – Take away that fool's bauble, the mace

**Come up and see me sometime** – Why don't you come up sometime, and see me?

**My lips are sealed** – My lips are not yet unsealed

---

## EXPRESSIONS OF DEEP GLOOM

Go deep
Touch bottom
Be on one's knees
Sink to the bottom,
Now the only way is up.

Plumb the depths
Reach rock bottom
Reach one's nadir
Plunge into despair

**FOUR EXERCISES TO HELP REDUCE A DOUBLE CHIN**

## WORDS WHICH HAVE ENTERED THE LANGUAGE AND THE DICTIONARY IN THE TWENTY-FIRST CENTURY

| | |
|---|---|
| CUL8R | text talk for see you later |
| Bi-curious | considering experimenting with bisexuality |
| Bifter | a cannabis cigarette |
| Booty call | a meeting arranged for the purpose of having sex |
| Bootylicious | sexually attractive, especially with curvaceous buttocks |
| Dad rock | often disparaging term for a type of music that tends to appeal to adults, often played by middle-aged musicians |
| Drunkathon | a session in which excessive quantities of alcohol are consumed |
| GR8 | great |
| LUV | love |
| Mixologist | a person who serves drinks, especially cocktails, at a bar |
| Noisenik | a rock musician who performs loud, harsh music |
| Shagtastic | sexually attractive, or excellent |
| Sobriety coach | a person who helps someone who has been dependent on alcohol or drugs to maintain an abstinent lifestyle |
| Yummy mummy | an attractive woman who has had children |
| Bodypacker | a person who smuggles illicit drugs in balloons, condoms or similar plastic bags which have been inserted somewhere about the body |
| Wan2tlk? | Do you want to talk? |

## PHRASES SPOKEN BY PARROTS

Pieces of eight (traditional pirate parrot)

Ahoy shipmates (as above)

Polly put the kettle on

Who's a pretty boy then?

B***er off you silly old fool

Help, help, murder! (guard parrot)

Who do you think you are?

All right, I'm coming (guard parrot)

---

## COUNT YOUR SINS

| | |
|---|---|
| the sin of a sailor | sinbad |
| sin of time | since |
| sin of honesty | sincerity |
| a mathematical sin | sine |
| sin of an easy job | sinecure |
| a muscular sin | sinew |
| sin to music | sing |
| sin in the East | Singapore |
| an only sin | single |
| double sin where bad men go | Sing-Sing |
| an unusual sin | singular |
| ominous sin | sinister |
| a sin to go down | sink |
| sin of a curve | sinuous |

## IMPORTANT LESSONS TO LEARN FROM THE MOVIES

You must pick up your phone after the first ring or the other person will assume you are out and hang up.

If you are in a high-speed car chase, you will always encounter the following obstacles; a blind man, a street vendor selling fruit, a one-way street, a pile of empty cardboard boxes, a wobbly old man on a bike carrying a string of onions, and a sign saying 'Bridge ahead incomplete'.

Move to New York as everyone there can afford huge apartments regardless of their income.

A pursuing car will not try to barge you off the road until immediately after you spot it in your rear-view mirror.

At least one of a pair of identical twins will be born evil.

Most laptop computers are powerful enough to override the communications system of any invading alien society.

If you are blonde and pretty it is still possible to become a world expert on nuclear fission at the age of twenty-two.

All grocery shopping bags contain at least one stick of French bread.

You are very likely to survive any battle in any war unless you make the mistake of showing someone a picture of your sweetheart back home.

A man will show no pain while taking the most terrific beating, but will wince when a woman tries to clean his wounds.

Even when driving down a perfectly straight road it is necessary to turn the steering wheel vigorously from left to right every few seconds.

If you are being chased in a city, you can usually blend into a crowd of carnival revellers.

## GOOD ADVICE

If you can smile when things go wrong, you already know who you are going to blame.

Before you criticize someone, walk a mile in their shoes. That way you are a mile away, and you have their shoes too.

When in doubt, mumble.

Gargle everyday to see if your throat leaks.

Before packing away your Christmas decorations, smash one of the lights. Next year, you will have no difficulty in discovering which bulb doesn't work.

Always remember, those who live by the sword get shot by those who don't.

Remember, too, that many people have fallen by the sword, but many more have fallen from a turned ankle.

---

## UNLIKELY FACTS

Panama hats are made in Ecuador

Catgut comes from sheep and horses

Russians celebrate the October Revolution in November

A camel-hair brush is made of squirrel fur

The Canary Islands in the Atlantic are named after dogs

King George V's first name was Albert

A purple finch is crimson

Chinese gooseberries come from New Zealand

# FAMOUS PEOPLE WITH FIRST NAMES AND SURNAMES THAT BEGIN WITH THE SAME LETTER

*Billy Bragg* – protest singer
*Simone Signoret* – actress
*Louis Lamour* – author of Western novels
*Charlotte Church* – child singer
*Steven Spielberg* – film director/producer
*Terry-Thomas* – actor
*Peter Purves* – Blue Peter presenter
*Marilyn Monroe* – actress
*Marilyn Manson* – rock performer
*Jasper Johns* – artist
*Lyle Lovett* – singer
*Vincent Van Gogh* – artist
*Pablo Picasso* – artist
*Walter Winterbottam* – first England football manager
*Eddie Edwards* – ski jumper
*Francis Ford Coppola* – film director/producer
*Heinrich Himmler* – prominent Nazi
*Howard Hughes* – multi-millionnaire
*Boris Becker* – tennis player
*Ernie Els* – golfer
*Doris Day* – actress
*Diana Dors* – actress
*Magnus Magnusson* – *Mastermind* presenter
*Malcolm Muggeridge* – journalist and sage
*Malcolm Marshall* – West Indian cricketer
*Arthur Ashe* – US tennis player
*Desmond Dekker* – musician
*Miriam Makeba* – musician
*William Wordsworth* – poet
*Wilbur Wright* – avationist
*Tina Turner* – singer
*Edward Elgar* – composer
*Greta Garbo* – actress
*Harry Houdini* – escapologist
*Graham Greene* – author

## FAMOUS PEOPLE WITH SURNAMES THAT ARE FIRST NAMES

Hank Marvin – musician
David Jason – actor
Calvin Pete – US golfer
Henry James – US novelist
Elton John – musician
Martha Stewart – US lifestyle guru
W. G. Grace – cricketer
D. H. Lawrence – author
T. E. Lawrence – of Arabia
Robert E. Lee – Confederate general
John Wayne – actor

## FAMOUS PEOPLE WHOSE NAME BEGINS WITH 'H' WHO ARE KNOWN BY THE ONE NAME

Hitler – German leader
Hannibal – Carthaginian elephant man
Horace – classical poet
Heidi – children's character
Henry (I to VIII) – kings of England
Homer – classical poet
Hippocrates – Ancient Greek doctor
Hammurabi – Babylonian king
Hypatia – female ancient Greek scholar
Hatshepsut – Egyptian queen

## FAMOUS PEOPLE WHOSE NAME BEGINS WITH 'S' WHO ARE KNOWN BY THE ONE NAME

Saladin – Arab leader
Socrates – philosopher
Solomon – King of Israel
Sosigenes – Egyptian astronomer

Sophocles – Greek playwright
Spartacus – leader of slave revolt
Spock – illogical
Sting – singer

## BRITISH FOOTBALL TEAM LAST NAMES

| | |
|---|---|
| United | Rangers |
| City | Thistle |
| Town | Athletic |
| Albion | County |
| Forest | Academicals |
| Argyle | Rovers |
| Orient | Hotspur |
| Alexandra | Wednesday |

---

## THE LONGEST ONE-SYLLABLE WORDS IN THE ENGLISH LANGUAGE

| | |
|---|---|
| scratched | screeched |
| scrounged | scrunched |
| straights | strengths |
| stretched | |

---

## SOME LATIN SWEAR WORDS

*irrumator* – b*****
*mentula* – penis
*meretrix* – whore
*podex* – bottom
*spucatum tauri* – bulls**t

---

## COUNTRIES WHOSE NAMES BEGIN AND END WITH THE SAME LETTER

| | |
|---|---|
| Algeria | Argentina |
| America | Angola |
| Australia | Austria |

## WELL-KNOWN BUNGEE-JUMPING SITES

Colorado River Bridge, Costa Rica

Danube Tower, Austria

Fairlop Waters, United Kingdom

'Goliath', Canada

Kawarau Suspension Bridge, New Zealand

Skipper's Canyon, New Zealand

Verzasca Dam, Switzerland

Victoria Falls, Africa

---

## FINGERNAILS

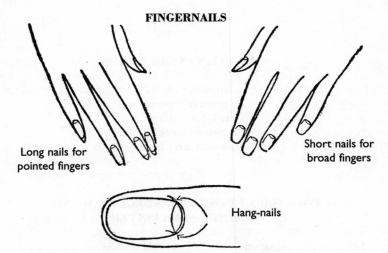

Long nails for
pointed fingers

Short nails for
broad fingers

Hang-nails

Shape your nails to suit your hands and personality. Hang-nails are
caused by dryness of the skin and should be treated with lanolin

## BISCUITS

Almond crunch
fingers
Anise cookies
Apple flapjacks
Austrian streusels
Bran shorties
Brownies
Caraway cookies
Cherry peel bars
Chocolate crunchies

Chocolate walnut
bars
Cinnamon biscuits
Coconut squares
Coffee drops
Digestives
Easter cookies
Finnish gingers
Ginger nuts
Golden oaties

Hazelnut clusters
Iced treats
Melting moments
Passion fruit squares
Parkin
Peanut crisps
Peanut chews
Viennese shells

---

## STRATEGIC MANAGEMENT BIBLE

In the Beginning was the Plan.
And then came the Assumptions.
And the Assumptions were without form.
And the Plan was completely without substance
   and the darkness was upon the face of the workers
   and they spoke among themselves, saying:
'It is a crock of s**t and it stinketh.'
And the workers went unto the Supervisors and sayeth:
'It is a pile of dung and none may abide the odour thereof.'
And the Supervisors went unto their Managers and sayeth unto them:
'It is a container of excrement and it is very strong,
   such that none may abide by it.'
And the Managers went unto their Directors and sayeth:
'It is a vessel of fertilizer, and none may abide its strength.'
And the Directors spoke amongst themselves, saying one to another:
'It contains that which aids plant growth, and it is very strong.'
And the Directors went unto CEO and sayeth unto him:
'It promotes growth and is very powerful.'
And the CEO went unto the Chairman and sayeth unto him:
'This new plan will actively promote the growth and efficiency
of this Organization, and in these areas in particular.'
And the Chairman looked upon the Plan, and saw that it was good,
   and the Plan became Policy.
This is How S**t Happens.

## OFFICE JARGON

1. **Blamestorming:** Sitting around in a group, discussing why a deadline was missed or a project failed, and who was responsible.

2. **Seagull Manager:** A manager who flies in, makes a lot of noise, poops all over everything and then leaves.

3. **Chainsaw Consultant:** An outside expert brought in to reduce the employee head count, leaving the top brass with clean hands.

4. **Cube Farm:** An office filled with cubicles.

5. **Idea Hamsters:** People who always seem to have their idea generators running.

6. **Prairie Dogging:** When someone yells or drops something loudly in a cube farm, and people's heads pop over the walls to see what's going on.

7. **Assmosis:** The process by which some people seem to absorb success and advancement by kissing up to the boss rather than working hard.

8. **Uninstalled:** Euphemism for being fired.

9. **Dehired, Downsizing, Decruitment:** Euphemisms for being fired.

10. **Depression:** anger without enthusiasm.

---

## TERMS OF ENDEARMENT

| | | | |
|---|---|---|---|
| Angel | Love | Chuck | Sweet thing |
| Angel eyes | Lovie | Sweetheart | Sweetiepie |
| Bunnikins | Lover | Sweetie | Wuffles |
| Cutie | Lovie dove | Sweet cheeks | Fluffy wuffy |
| Dear | My love | Sweetums | Petit choux |
| Dearest | Ducks | Honey | |
| Darling | Duckie | Honeybun | |

## A FIRST-AID KIT FOR DOGS

thermometer
tin of meat essence
measuring glass
antiseptic gauze and wool
bandages
liniment
castor oil capsules
powders for sickness

diarrhoea mixture of prepared
chalk
antidotes for poisoning
tincture of aconite
whisky
ipecacuanha wine
olive oil
sulphate of magnesia

---

## SOME OF THE COMMONEST WORDS
## IN THE ENGLISH LANGUAGE

| in | you | with | to | are |
| is | it | the | his | have |
| from | was | of | be | they |
| had | as | and | for | not |
| at | on | a | I | or |

---

## AND NOW...

Close
Conclusion
Payoff
Last round
Last stretch
Last gasp
Swan song
Envoi
Coda
Finish
Period
THE END

## INDEX

The reader anxious to furnish his copy of this book with an adequate index will, we trust, take comfort upon finding, on this very page, that, unlike so many of today's publishers, we regard an index as being central to a reader's individual taste. It follows, therefore, that it is no part of our task to foist upon the public some work of indexing that will almost certainly, and in almost every respect, fall short of a reader's actual wants. Indeed not: for what is clearly wanted is an index tailored precisely to each individual, since not only will the reader then be able to find his way around his cherished copy in exactly the manner, and with precisely the facility, that he wishes, but he will learn a new skill, one that he may be able to put to use for pleasure, and perhaps even for profit.

We are not yet, however, so steeped in commercialism as not to extend to the eager reader the helping hand of experience as he embarks upon his virgin task as an indexer. This takes the form of two pieces of advice: namely, first, that an index should be compiled in alphabetical order; and, second, entries that contain several page references should list those references in ascending order of page number. A single example of the latter should suffice: 'Intercourse, sexual, incidence of among small rodents, 9, 27–9, 118 ff., 143 n., 406'.

As to alphabetical order, it is no part of our duties to encourage too great a rigidity. Thus 'Popular assault rifles' may be so indexed, or as 'Rifles, assault, popular', or as 'Assault rifles, popular', according to taste or prejudice. This also allows of a degree of cross-referencing, viz.: 'Assault rifles, popular, *see* Popular assault rifles'; 'Popular assault rifles, *see* Rifles, assault, popular', et cetera; a system which has the merit of massively increasing the extent of an index.

In conclusion, it remains only to thank the reader for having borne with us thus far, and to wish him every success, as well as pleasure and the satisfaction of a job well done, as he begins his abecedarian journey.

THE PUBLISHERS